Politicizing Digital Space:
Theory, the Internet, and Renewing Democracy

Trevor Garrison Smith

University of Westminster Press
www.uwestminsterpress.co.uk

Competing interests

The author declares that they have no competing interests in publishing this book

Published by
University of Westminster Press
101 Cavendish Street
London W1W 6XH
www.uwestminsterpress.co.uk

First published 2017
Series cover concept: Mina Bach (minabach.co.uk)
Cover Design: tbc

Printed and bound by CPI Group (UK) Ltd, Croydon, CR0 4YY

Print and digital versions typeset by Siliconchips Services Ltd.

ISBN (Paperback): 978-1-911534-40-2
ISBN (PDF): 978-1-911534-41-9
ISBN (EPUB): 978-1-911534-42-6
ISBN (Mobi): 978-1-911534-43-3

DOI: https://doi.org/10.16997/book5

The full text of this book has been peer-reviewed to ensure high
academic standards. For full review policies, see:
http://www.uwestminsterpress.co.uk/site/publish/

Suggested citation:
Smith, T. G. 2017. *Politicizing Digital Space: Theory, The Internet, and
Renewing Democracy*. London: University of Westminster Press. DOI: https://
doi.org/10.16997/book5. License: CC-BY-NC-ND 4.0

To read the free, open access version of this book
online, visit https://doi.org/10.16997/book5 or
scan this QR code with your mobile device: 

Contents

CHAPTER 1

Introduction

In the wake of the so-called 'Arab Spring,' Occupy, and Anonymous movements, attention has increasingly been paid to the intersection of politics and the internet. In the popular media, commentators such as Roger Cohen of the *New York Times* took a technological determinist approach, as he declared Facebook founder Mark Zuckerberg to be the true leader of the protests spreading across North Africa (Cohen 2011). The internet was positioned as causing the protests, as technological modernity was positioned as bringing with it political modernity, thus leading to the overthrow of long-standing dictatorships. Against this technological determinist view, many scholars swung to the opposite side of the spectrum and declared that the internet was not really important at all, and positioned it as merely another useful tool among many for political activists (Burris 2011). What is missing from these two positions is an appreciation of what the internet could mean for a reinvigorated idea of politics itself. These movements are interesting not simply because they used social networks and mobile phones as part of their protests, but because they demonstrated some of the latent possibilities of using the internet to usher in a new form of radically democratic politics.

While I will argue that the internet is more than a useful tool for protesters, the biggest obstacle to establishing a new form of online politics is not technological but political. Too often, theorists take the idea of politics for granted without discussing what it means. This theoretical confusion has led people to claim that everything is political, thus diminishing the specificity and value of politics as a concept, or has led the public to equate politics with the exercise of authority by government. In this sense, politics is now seen by many as simply a dirty word, as something to avoid and distance oneself from. As Colin Hay points out, we have gotten to the point where the word politics is now used as a term of derision in every day speech, as to 'label an activity or process "political" is, it seems, invariably to deride and distance oneself from it' (Hay 2007, 5).

How to cite this book chapter:

Smith, T. G. 2017. *Politicizing Digital Space: Theory, The Internet, and Renewing Democracy.* Pp. 1–9. London: University of Westminster Press. DOI: https://doi. org/10.16997/book5.a. License: CC-BY-NC-ND 4.0

All of the aspects of the internet which might help enhance political space and improve engagement will be lost if the concept of politics as something worthwhile and empowering is abandoned. We cannot talk about new forms of online politics enthusiastically when people have given up on politics altogether.

Traditional structures of authority have increasingly begun to fail in recent years. Not only did the Arab Spring come out of nowhere to bring down what seemed liked eternal dictatorships, but traditional structures of authority within representative democracies have begun to come under attack as well, as people continue to turn against 'politics.' In the extraordinary 2016 United States election campaign, the rise of Bernie Sanders and Donald Trump ushered in a serious challenge to the American party establishment of the Democrats and Republicans. The loss of trust in the traditional party power structures opened the door for these two outsider candidates. Trump's strong support from the working class in the de-industrialized Rust Belt is a sign of the failure of the authority of traditional unions, as they have lost their power to organize the working class politically. The 2016 election also can be viewed as a failure of the traditional authority of the corporate media establishment. Trump was able to manipulate media coverage so that he was continually the focus, while at the same time instilling a sense of distrust towards the mainstream media in his supporters. The election of Trump, the victory of the Leave campaign in the Brexit referendum of 2016, and the rise of the alt-right or post-fascism (see Tamas 2000 for an insightful overview of post-fascism as a political philosophy) demonstrate rejections of 'politics' from the right. From the left, the election of Syriza in Greece in 2015, the new-found popularity of Bernie Sanders in 2016 and the election of Jeremy Corbyn as leader of the British Labour Party in 2015, along with the Occupy Wall Street movement entering the public consciousness in 2011 were all rejections of the traditional political establishment as well.

These rejections of establishment 'politics' should be interpreted as a rejection not of politics itself, but of a latent, although unarticulated, desire for more politics. Many political theorists, ranging from Chantal Mouffe to Slavoj Žižek, have recently described the status quo in Europe and North America as post-political, a point that was being made by Hannah Arendt as early as the 1950s. The problem was not that politics has become oppressive, but that we simply lack avenues for politics altogether. In recent years, the neoliberal consensus ushered in an era where even social democratic political parties adopted neoliberal economics under the so-called Third Way. The recent events just described represent an undoing of this post-political neoliberal consensus as well as a desire to throw a wrench into the standard operating procedures of representative democracy. While people want to break this anti-political status quo, and are doing so by rejecting establishment politicians and traditional power structures, these repressed desires for more politics can also be dangerous if they lack actual political avenues of expression and simply become a call for further depoliticizations.

Without a positive vision for what politics could be when it is freed from the shackles of representative government or mere reactive protest, this popular uprising against the establishment can easily be channelled into post-fascist movements which harness the desire for change into an even more insidious form of anti-politics. The Arab Spring movement swapped a dictator for an elected Islamist government which was then overthrown by the military, making it a true full-turn revolution. The rejection of establishment politics and the decline of the neoliberal consensus has led to the election of Donald Trump and new popularity for other post-fascist leaders such as Marine Le Pen in France. There is a popular desire globally for a new way of doing and being political which moves beyond both the alienating structures of representation and the simply reactive forms of oppositional politics which has become overly focused on victimization and identity. A positive conception of politics as empowering and participatory is required to prevent this anti-establishment sentiment from becoming the grounds for something worse. It is the contention of this book that to reinvigorate the idea of politics, it must go online in order to find new spaces and modes of being political that are unavailable offline. The goal is to articulate a theory of politics that is realizable with the help of the internet, thus making politics something that can be actively worked towards and not merely a far off dream.

The internet is no longer new or strange, but is now simply a normal part of our lives. In the early days of theorizing the internet, there was a feeling that the internet held radical potential to change everything about our political structures. As the current trend of cyberscepticism is keen to remind us, those early ideas about the internet transforming everything have failed to materialize. The cybersceptics tend to overstate their case, however, and in the process make the same mistake as the cyberutopians when they make claims about 'The Internet' as a whole. The internet is not a monolith, and thus being utopian or sceptical about its potential makes little sense. It is time to move beyond somewhat simplistic ideas of talking about the internet as if there was only way to use it and only one type of website. It is time to look at the internet as a collection of different websites, applications, and hardware configurations and thus realize that any statement about The Internet being political is as meaningless as speaking about the political suitability of planet Earth. The primary interest in the internet for the purposes of this book is precisely that online space is so malleable. The internet is interesting and necessary for reinvigorating politics because it can provide possibilities for beginning something new. New websites and applications can be created which can help facilitate various aspects of politics in a way that is simply not possible offline. Thus the argument of this book links politics to the internet because, as Arendt argued, politics is inherently about beginning something new, which today is most easily accomplished online.

Both left and right responses to the lack of politics that are driving anti-establishment sentiment have failed to lead to any real change. Despite my enthusiasm for Occupy Wall Street and the Arab Spring, both movements failed to put forward an alternative vision which could lead to real change. They were successful movements but only insofar as they were reactive: yes, we were all opposed to the dictators in Egypt and Tunisia and were opposed to the 1% around the world, but neither of these movements had any success in articulating alternatives. The same can be said for the newfound anti-establishment post-fascist movements. They have been successful in rallying people against some of the more excessive elements of neoliberal globalization and have harnessed popular sentiment against neoliberal technocrats, but their alternative to the status quo is an even deeper form of depoliticization. Both sides have engaged with creating political space online, which as many scholars have outlined (see for example Fuchs 2014, Milan 2015, Atton 2006), provide a few nascent examples of how a new form of politics can operate online. What is needed is to take these examples as a starting point, and consider the wider theoretical idea of how to use the internet to be political in a way that moves beyond both unsustainable street protests and the election of populist representatives. This book seeks to develop a theoretical account of some of the primary issues such a new form of online politics will face. This is not a book about how political activists currently use the internet, but instead is about how political theory can help us think ahead in order to address the sort of problems and arguments that arise when we seek to be political online.

In order to create online spaces that can facilitate more political engagement, we need a clear understanding of what we mean by politics, especially in relation to its opposing force of anti-politics. The political theory of Hannah Arendt is somewhat unique in that she takes politics as its own domain of human activity seriously. For Arendt, politics is not merely the exercise of state authority or a subfield of economics or ethics. Politics is what makes us free, rather than what oppresses us, and it is precisely this positive connotation of politics that must be reinvigorated. Arendt's political theory is attractive precisely because she views politics as beneficial in its own right, and not a mere means to some other end. If the existing anti-political deadlock is to be broken, activists must seek to reinvigorate politics, rather than escape it. In addition to drawing on Arendt's theoretical framework for an empowering rather than oppressing understanding of politics, there is a growing group of contemporary thinkers who are seeking to reclaim politics as a specific and serious activity. I will place these contemporary theorists in a supporting role to the central figure of Arendt.

While it can be difficult to lump groups of diverse theorists together, thinkers such as Jacques Rancière, Chantal Mouffe, and Slavoj Žižek have been actively attempting to reclaim politics as precisely what is needed to bring change. This group of thinkers actively position themselves against the reduction of politics to state-based administration common among mainstream liberal and conservative thinkers as well as against the postmodern left who dissolve the specificity of politics into the critique of differential power relations. Politics as the state or politics as differential power relations ends up creating deeply anti-political attitudes in which the political is equated with restrictions on freedom. For the neoliberal, politics as state administration oppresses the free market and individual, and for the postmodern leftist, politics is an unequal power relation which generates the oppression of minorities. In both cases, politics is positioned as a problem to be overcome.

While Rancière, Žižek, and Mouffe are important contemporary figures because they are shifting the conversation toward viewing politics as something worthwhile, the work of Arendt on this measure stands above them all and often seems just as, if not more, relevant to contemporary issues than the work of those alive today. After writing *On the Origins of Totalitarianism*, a book with a pessimistic undertone that sees totalitarian impulses seeping into all forms of government, Arendt witnessed the events of the Hungarian uprising against Soviet rule in 1956 which spurred her to write *The Human Condition* and *The Promise of Politics*. These two books are primarily concerned with the value of politics and its ability to create something new in order to break from even the most oppressive anti-political situation. Against the backdrop of today's general hostility to politics, Arendt stands out as a staunch defender of politics in a way that demands contemporary attention.

Arendt's reception in contemporary scholarship is varied and complex, reflective of her own varied and complex thought. While there is a body of scholarship that focuses on her defence of politics,[1] Arendt is often invoked in ways that are antithetical to her commitment to politics. As Kalyvas points out, there is a

> trend in Arendt scholarship that is gradually moving away from the political qualities of her writings. Today she is read more as a philosopher and a moral thinker rather than as a political theorist concerned predominantly with the secular realm of appearances (2009, 188).

The recent edited collection on Arendt's thought for the occasion of her 100th birthday *Thinking in Dark Times* demonstrates this trend (Berkowitz, Katz, and Keenan, 2009). The bulk of the essays in the book treat Arendt's thought outside of and even in some cases against her explicitly political concerns. Theorists such as Seyla Benhabib (1992) interpret Arendt as an advocate of consensus rather than as the staunch defender of agonistic politics she actually was. Such interpretations have spread and have even led prominent proponents of agonistic politics, such as Chantal Mouffe (2005, 8), to engage in polemics against Arendt as a supposed supporter of eliminating political conflict. Žižek (2010) and Rancière (2004) also engage with Arendt only with respect to her definition of totalitarianism and concept of human rights, again underscoring this trend where Arendt is recast as a moral philosopher, despite her continued insistence that she was not a philosopher but in fact a political theorist. These depictions of Arendt as hostile to the project of recovering politics by this group of political theorists are all the more remarkable because of how much they share with

Arendt's core project of asserting the value of politics. In reading these contemporary thinkers as an extension of Arendt's thoughts about the promise of politics, I am seeking to reassert Arendt's proper position as a political thinker and demonstrate her sometimes obscured influence on these thinkers, while also using these contemporary thinkers to make up for some of her limitations.

At the same time, the theories of these thinkers have been around for awhile, yet have failed to inspire confidence in a political alternative to the anti-political status quo, not just in the wider population but even among activists. After the fall of long standing dictatorships in North Africa, the response to the question of what came next was representative democracy, not as an enthusiastic victory that activists had been fighting for, but more as a kind default answer for lack of any better ideas. It is on this register, however, that we need to reinvigorate political theory by pushing an engagement with the internet. To digitize political theory is to re-examine the work of Arendt and the others for ways in which new avenues of application may be opened up by emerging technologies. While Mouffe and Žižek have expressed hesitation with respect to the prospect for online democracy, and Rancière has said next to nothing on the topic, Arendt has traditionally been interpreted as being somewhat sceptical of the prospects for politics in relation to technology. Arendt begins *The Human Condition* with an analysis of the launching of Sputnik, which she fears is ushering in the ultimate form of alienation which could render politics impossible. What she did not realize was that satellites would become part of a global communications network which has the potential to greatly enhance the ability for people to directly engage politically with each other.

The argument of this book rests on the idea that politics as a concept and practice can be reinvigorated by both digitizing the political and politicizing the digital. Political theory can help restore the poor reputation of politics but only if it appears relevant to our daily lives. We can theorize radical democracies and new forms of participatory decision making, but without the technological aspect that presents a real path toward implementation, such theorizing comes across as disconnected from reality. At the same time, much of the literature that focuses on the internet from the perspective of communication theory and political economy tends to lack a proper engagement with the notion of the political. The fact that political activists might use social media to organize with other activists or that these social media platforms are owned by large corporations are interesting aspects of the interaction of politics and the internet, but are somewhat narrow concerns without a proper account of what it means to be political in the first place. This book does not simply assume that politics is obvious enough to not need an explanation, but instead focuses primarily on providing a theoretical account of what politics is and how it is complicated by placing it online.

To develop this point that politics itself needs an explanation in order to make sense of how politics can operate online, I argue that politics can be defined in terms of four terrains of contestation (public space, subjectivity, participation, and conflict), which act as sliding scales between political and anti-political configurations of a situation. While this makes politics as an overarching concept harder to define, as it consists of configuring public space, subjectivity, participation, and conflict in ways that are more political than anti-political, it can allow us to use these four terrains to make judgements about whether a situation is political or not. Since each terrain is a sliding scale from political to anti-political, the terrains can be used as both evaluative criteria and as sites of action, as the goal is to push each terrain toward a more political configuration. Rather than simply setting out a definition of politics as a whole, and leaving a question mark on how to get from here to there, adopting these four terrains as sliding scales means that action toward politicization can be more concretely envisioned.

Each chapter will focus on one of these terrains and both argue for why configuring it in a more political fashion is superior to an anti-political configuration, and how the internet can help achieve the goal of increased politicization. The internet will also be a complicating factor in many terrains, as simply placing politics online does not automatically lead to more politicization. I persistently argue that the internet is malleable and open to different configurations, given that the software layer allows the creation of new spaces and the reprogramming of old ones. Again, it is important to remember that when I speak of the internet, I am referring to a collection of websites, hardware configurations, and different possible uses. Thus the focus is on how to use the internet to bring about more politicization while at the same time being aware that the internet can be used in many depoliticizing ways as well.

In the chapters that follow I will develop the argument that Arendt and the group of contemporary thinkers mentioned earlier can provide a theoretical ground for understanding a technologically enabled politics. In a time when the political realm is considered an exclusive space divorced from everyday life, we can build an online political realm that is readily accessible at all times. In the face of the state's continuing operations to place people in identity boxes which mark them as unqualified to take part in politics, we can enter online spaces which disrupt identity and qualification in a radical way. When participation in public affairs is deemed too complicated or impossible for the average person, we can go online to engage and participate in unofficial forms of politics at the same time as millions of other people. When consensus has become a reigning idyll and dissent is seen not as the basis of politics but as something disruptive of it, the internet provides outlets for the expression and organization of dissent and conflicting opinions. Considered together, the internet is not simply something helpful or useful for a reinvigorated politics, but is the space within which the reinvigoration of politics will take place.

In order to make this argument, the next chapter will deal with the terrain of the political realm in terms of what it entails and how placing it online can be beneficial. Against anti-political attempts to deny the need for any defined political space and against the weaker arguments in favour of a public sphere, I position the political realm as a necessity for the commonality of politics. In order to be political, we need a protected space to exercise our political freedom in a positive sense. When thinking of how we interact online, it becomes clear that the internet is not just a technological object or tool, but a new form of space. Online space opens up a whole host of new ways of being and interacting, which can also call into existence new ways of being political. By placing such a political realm online, it both enables easy access to such a realm and generates debates about the political status of the body. I argue that politics is not a collection of mute bodies but a network of relationships based on the ideas and actions of people, so that what matters is not physical proximity but the capacity to engage with others in such a way to allow the kinds of debate and action that are essential if politics is to flourish. The chapter goes on to contrast the anti-political social realm with the political realm in terms of various websites and seeks to distinguish between hardware and software layers online, thus presenting a case against essentialist arguments that the internet as a whole is this or that way.

Having presented how a political realm should operate, I then move to the question of what it means to be political within such a space. Chapter three takes as its starting point the renewed interest in theorizing political subjectivity as universal and places it in contrast to anti-political attempts to assert various forms of particularized social identity. Given that such theories of subjectivity do not posit a set of universal values that an individual must adhere to in order to become a political subject, but in fact aim for a stripping away of all such properties to ensure universality is empty, the way people interact in online political discussion forums naturally lends itself to this political subjectivization process. The new forms of space that are created online can lead to new ways of being political and new forms of political subjectivity that may not have made sense in the pre-internet era. While many have taken issue with the idea of a disembodied online political subjectivity, I argue that disembodiment and pseudonymity are the greatest strengths of the online political subject because it helps undermine the dominance of identity in physical space which places so much emphasis on bodies being represented. The representation of bodies not only leads to huge problems with respect to discrimination in the form of racism, sexism, and homophobia, but it also entrenches alienating political systems which aim to represent bodies rather than give voice to individual subjects. Such a discussion of online subjectivity leads to questions about how Arendt's concept of subjectivity as revealing oneself might operate within the often bodiless and anonymous fluctuations of online space.

With an understanding of how to become a political subject within the political realm, chapter four is concerned with the activities of these subjects in the political realm. My argument is that participation is one of the most basic requirements for politics, as the ability to speak and be heard and to take part in action is essential for any attractive understanding of politics. Anti-political strategies seek to deflect participation away from the political realm or minimize it to extreme infrequency such as through voting for representatives. Participation in society is framed anti-politically as having a job and paying taxes, which promotes a form of political passivity in favour of economic activity. The internet presents a challenge to these anti-political models by making political participation extremely accessible, and thus undermining the classic argument against participatory democracy that there is not enough time or space for any but a select few to take part in politics. The internet can also facilitate deeper forms of participation, which move beyond the simplistic demands for referendums which so often simply empower the mob rather than enabling serious forms of engagement.

The fifth chapter will engage with the terrain of conflict, which naturally arises when unique political subjects participate in speech and action inside a political realm. I argue that conflict is an inevitable outcome of the basic fact of human plurality and that it is the primary driver of politics. Conflict is valuable and inevitable, and having a political outlet for conflict is necessary in order to prevent it from escalating into violence. In this manner, politics is a kind of 'talking cure' for conflict that allows people to voice their disagreements and try to persuade others of their opinion without having to result to violent force. The internet presents an interesting dilemma for theorists of agonistic politics, as on the one hand it can facilitate political conflict as it is much easier to not only find people with other points of view but to disagree with them without any fear of the disagreement turning violent, while, on the other hand the internet can facilitate filter bubbles and lead to various forms of uncivil speech which depoliticize conflict. Questions thus arise about whether the internet allows anyone to become Socrates, questioning the views of everyone else and making society better by causing people to think about their own beliefs, or whether it turns everyone into the Socrates as seen by his accusers who was simply a social nuisance engaged in a primitive form of trolling which seeks to cause annoyance and conflict without a higher purpose.

The internet on its own obviously will not solve our problems for us by magically bringing about new forms of more engaged political practice. At the same time, however, any attempt to reinvigorate politics must find its home online or risk simply coming across as old fashioned and as yet another attempt to dream up theoretical solutions with no real path toward implementation. The internet is now a normal part of our lives, but this does not mean that it has to be seen as drained of any radical potential. While the internet is not new, it still contains an enormous amount of untapped possibility that could change the way we think about what politics should be and about what types of politics are possible.

CHAPTER 2

The Political Realm

2.1 What is the Place of Politics?

The question of where politics can take place, is in many ways, the core problem of conceptualizing an internet enabled politics. Yet, before we can question whether politics can be located online, there are questions and disputes over where it can be located offline. Under the conditions of modern government, and within popular and mainstream political science, the location of politics is generally considered to be the exclusive domain of legislative or executive authority. The people inside such an exclusive understanding of the political realm are there because they meet a qualification, either of being elected or appointed. Before we can even begin to question whether politics might be able to be placed online, the question of whether or not politics can occur outside of these limited and exclusive institutions of official government must be considered. The first task consists in asking what exactly the political realm consists of, and asking how it might function outside of the official spaces of governmental authority. The answer consists of conceiving of a political realm as an open space of freedom and appearance for all. While there have been many conceptualizations of such a political realm, and I take Hannah Arendt's depiction as a theoretical basis, the implementation of full-fledged political realms of this nature have either fallen far short of the theory or have lived extremely brief lives. The internet, however, presents a new hope for a robust political realm as it involves a new kind of space that is less prone to both forceful dismissals by those who wish to constrain politics, and also lacks the physical obstacles that have challenged previous attempts to build an offline political realm.

The significance of the problem of the political realm, or rather lack of one, is perhaps best demonstrated by how the Occupy movement and the activists in Tunisia and Egypt attempted to create their own spaces of political circulation. These spaces were meant to not just communicate a message of opposition to

---

How to cite this book chapter:

Smith, T. G. 2017. *Politicizing Digital Space: Theory, The Internet, and Renewing Democracy*. Pp. 11–40. London: University of Westminster Press. DOI: https://doi. org/10.16997/book5.b. License: CC-BY-NC-ND 4.0

the government, but to enable and put into practice an alternative arrangement which, to some degree, was meant to establish a political realm open to all. The fact that the most common and effective means of protesting the state comes from establishing alternative political spaces speaks to the frustration that people feel from being structurally excluded from the official realm of government proceedings. These movements are particularly interesting examples precisely because they used the internet to expand their temporary political realms beyond the site of physical protests and out into the global cyberspace. It then became possible to enter the political space of these protests without actually physically being in New York, Cairo, or Tunis, demonstrating the potential of the internet as a site of politics to truly open up the political realm to anyone who wishes to take part.

The importance of the political realm relates to its publicity, as politics is an inherently collective affair. Without a recognized place to go to engage with other people and perform politics, any attempt to act politically becomes futile and isolated. If one wishes to have a political impact, performing isolated actions that affect no one else simply fail to be of any political relevance. The need to theorize a political realm runs against the idea that everything is political, an idea which would attempt to imbue isolated personal acts with political significance. As Jodi Dean points out, ethical acts restricted to the scope of the personal have no political impact, and as she succinctly puts it, 'Goldman-Sachs doesn't care if you raise chickens in your backyard' (*The Communist Horizon with Jodi Dean* 2011). Making a difference politically requires engaging with other people, and the general problem today is that no such common place for politics exists, with the official spaces extremely exclusive and limited to politicians, and the unofficial spaces fragmented and lacking in publicity.

Given the importance of having a public place in which to engage in politics, this chapter makes the argument that a robust political realm, inspired by the work of Arendt, is amenable to being placed online, and, as such, the political realm as both an idea and practice can be rejuvenated. Online space can enable a more open political realm, as it need not be constrained by the traditional impediments of physical space and time, and thus can challenge arguments which seek to limit access to the political realm for allegedly practical reasons. The internet as a space is inherently everywhere, especially with the continued proliferation of wireless and cellular networks, which can make it practically available in a way that is impossible with offline space. Arendt's theorization of the political realm as a web of relations, as a realm of 'whos' rather than 'whats,' and as not requiring a fixed physical space are interpreted as providing a theoretical justification for performing politics online.

2.2 The Political Realm as Human Artifice

The primary need for a political realm lies in its commonality. Action in the political sense involves other people, as to live outside of politics requires one to be either a beast or a god, as Aristotle put it (Aristotle 1985, 37). The content of politics is the affairs of people living together; an isolated person has no need for politics, because no conflicts of opinion on the best course of action will arise. The political realm, however, is a world of human creation and does not arise naturally just because people live in close proximity. In this sense politics is not 'natural,' as it does not simply occur automatically, but requires conscious effort to build a realm where decisions can ideally be debated equally by all. Structures of force which rely on the logic of command and obey, or those which are modelled on the relation of the stronger to the weaker are not political and are not necessarily even uniquely human (Arendt 1998, 22–23). Hierarchies of natural ability or the force of the stronger are found throughout the animal world, but the construction of a world of equality is a political and specifically human invention.

Against the naturalistic attempts to ground politics in the structure of the family, Arendt emphasizes that the political realm provides a second public life beyond one's private family life (Arendt 1998, 24). This is a point that both Arendt and Jacques Rancière emphasize, in that the political realm in ancient Athens arose precisely from the reforms of Cleisthenes which abolished the organized units based on kinship that had formed the basis of Athenian government prior to the advent of democracy (Arendt 1998, 24). Arendt's focus on the political realm as an artificial construction of human activity is supported by Rancière's insistence that the political realm must be invented by abolishing the natural divisions of family, tribe, or wealth in favour of wholly artificial divisions drawn by the people (Rancière 2010a, 6). Rancière even goes so far as to argue that this is the defining characteristic of political democracy: that it 'consists above all in the act of revoking the law of birth and that of wealth; in affirming the pure contingency whereby individuals and populations come to find themselves in this or that place; in the attempt to build a common world on the basis of that sole contingency' (Rancière 2010a, 6).

The artificially constructed common world of the political realm depends on the plurality of perspectives offered by those who take part. In both Arendt and Rancière's conceptions, there is no natural ground for anyone to claim rulership, thus decisions on public affairs remain open to anyone and everyone. The commonality of the political realm is what guarantees the reality of the world, as despite the plurality of different opinions, they are all focused on a common object (Arendt 1998, 58). In this sense, the political realm brings people together, but also separates them. When people come together to engage in politics the content of their speech and action relates to the objects held in common between them. Arendt describes the political realm as akin to a table: it provides a common object which people gather around, but also provides a means of separation so that the people are not directly exposed to each other (Arendt 1998, 53). In a similar manner, Rancière describes political being-together as a being-between, in that political action can happen within the political realm, not only among those who view the same object from a different perspective, but also between worlds. Those who are denied access to the political realm can come together to open a dispute about the commonality of the political realm itself (Rancière 1999, 137). Given that such a conception of the political realm does not rely on the foundational beliefs of god, superiority of birth, or money as the measure of all things, there is no objective measure to appeal to in order to decide political matters. Politics exists precisely because no objective measure can be appealed to in order to make decisions. The constant offering of different opinions on controversial matters for which there is no obvious single solution is what continues to guarantee the reality of the public realm, a reality which cannot exist in private and requires other people for confirmation (Arendt 1998, 57).

By having a collective place where people can go to publicly present their view of the world to others, the political realm is common but also individualizing. To show who one really is by presenting one's unique perspective on the world allows the political actor to distinguish him or herself as a unique individual (Arendt 1998, 141). Without the political realm as a space of appearance which provides a space to excel and prove oneself as different from others, we are thrown into a faceless mass (Arendt 1998, 49). Too often the desire to distinguish oneself turns into a futile attempt to accumulate wealth when the political realm is lacking, often with harmful consequences for the public good as economic inequality becomes valorized. To distinguish oneself as a unique individual requires a realm of equals, as hierarchical structures exclude the majority from appearing politically, forcing them into the shadows.

The political realm as a space where people can distinguish themselves means that it is a space of conflict and dissensus, not only between each other and their conflicting opinions but on a structural level, in terms of who gets to enter the political realm, what their status is, and what topics can be discussed. In this sense, Rancière's notion of politics as disrupting the harmony of hierarchically assigned places complements Arendt's concept of the political sphere (Rancière 1999, 28). The political realm is never strictly separate or disconnected from the private or social spheres, as the political realm will never be pure in the sense that it has no exclusions. Issues and actors will inevitably need to initiate political acts to overcome unjust barriers that prevent entrance into the political realm. Arendt's desire to keep politics pure and clearly separate from the other realms of life has the tendency to depopulate 'the political stage by sweeping aside its always-ambiguous actors' (Rancière 2004, 301–302). While Rancière overstates his case against Arendt by arguing that her desire for political purity results in her concept of the political realm being nothing more than the exercise of state power, Arendt's concern is directed more toward what happens inside the political realm than toward those who may need to act politically to overcome unnecessary barriers. In her treatment of the poor with regards to the French Revolution for example, she argues that the problem of poverty is simply non-political, and could not be solved by the political 'process of decision and persuasion' (Arendt 2006b, 81). However as Bonnie Honig points out, Arendt argues that the boundless nature of political action often surprised its actors, opening the possibility that contemporary struggles related to who might be included within the political realm might have surprised Arendt as well (Honig 1993, 119).

By opening the boundaries of the political realm to dispute and dissensus, I do not mean to challenge the distinctness of the necessity for politics to have its own space, but only to express dissatisfaction with Arendt's more limited notion of the political realm, which would, for example, exclude economics as a political concern. In addition to a common political realm where actors can distinguish themselves as unique individuals in the Arendtian sense, there can be ad hoc political realms which open up sites of dissensus in the Rancièrian sense. Rancière's political realm arises in the gap between formal declarations of rights and the polemic about their verification, and thus the political realm for Rancière is a space of verifying and exercising the freedoms guaranteed by constitutional frameworks (Rancière 2004, 307). While, for Arendt, the political actor is already among his or her peers and distinguishes him or herself with great speeches and deeds undertaken with and against others, for Rancière the political actor distinguishes him or herself as a unique individual by testing the ability to act as an Arendtian actor. If that ability cannot be properly exercised, a dispute is opened which allows individuals to perform great deeds in the form of testing and practicing a right, which is formally guaranteed, but not being applied. In this sense, someone such as Rosa Parks would be the quintessential Rancièrian political actor who distinguishes herself by testing and enacting equality. Both of these aspects are essential to a proper conception of the political realm, and despite the disagreement between Rancière and Arendt, I will continue to hold their concepts of the political realm as complementary, as one requires the other to properly function.

2.3 The Web of Relations and the Three Layer Model of the Political Realm

What sustains the reality and interconnectedness of the political realm is not bodies assembled in a single place but the web of relations that is generated by political speech and action. The political realm is generated from people coming together to speak and act politically so that 'its true space lies between people living together for this purpose, no matter where they happen to be' (Arendt 1998, 198). Zuccotti Park became a political realm because people used it as a meeting space to come together in political speech and action, even though normally it is a rather bland concrete park with no political purpose. At the same time, an officially designated political space in which people do not come together in speech and action is not automatically political just because it has been labelled as such. As Benhabib argues, an Arendtian political realm 'is not a space in any topographical or institutional sense: a town hall or a city square where people do not 'act in concert' is not a public space in this Arendtian sense' (Benhabib 1993, 102). The web of relations formed by people acting together politically has the power to create political spaces.

Having a determined location where people can meet, as was the case with Tahrir Square for the Egyptian activists during the Arab Spring or Zuccotti Park for Occupy Wall Street, enables the concentration of energy needed for politics. While this location need not be a literal physical location, as web sites function in a similar manner, it does create boundaries so we know where to go to be political (Arendt 1998, 190). Emphasizing the unpredictability and boundlessness of political action, Arendt also argues in favour of the importance of constitutions as providing the framework to establish a positive space of freedom in the form of a political realm (Arendt 2006b, 227). The political realm can be described as having three layers, with the action of the people on the top being the most important, followed by a framework below of either formal law (such as in a constitution) or informal rules (which often determine how decisions are made during a protest), and finally at the bottom layer a location where people go to act politically (see figure 1).

While Arendt emphasizes that the bottom two layers are not part of the action of politics, they can be considered as constitutive of the political realm itself. Before politics can happen, 'a definite space had to be secured and a structure built where all subsequent actions could take place, the space being the public realm of the *polis* and its structure the law' (Arendt 1998, 195). Thus the bottom two layers have a pre-political nature, but are still part of the structure of the actual political realm. As Christian Volk points out, the law has the quality of structuring the process of politics in a way that should facilitate the formation of political relationships (Volk 2010). Politics needs a human artifice to house it, as without this common political realm, 'human affairs would be as floating, as futile and vain, as the wanderings of nomad tribes' (Arendt 1998, 204). Even though Arendt is keen to emphasize that the political realm is not a physical location but the organization of people acting together, as demonstrated by her comment that it was not Athens but the Athenians who were the *polis*, political action does need a common space, otherwise it devolves into the futile attempts to engage in politics alone (Arendt 1998, 195). By describing the political realm as having three layers, it becomes apparent that a defined space, rules, and the

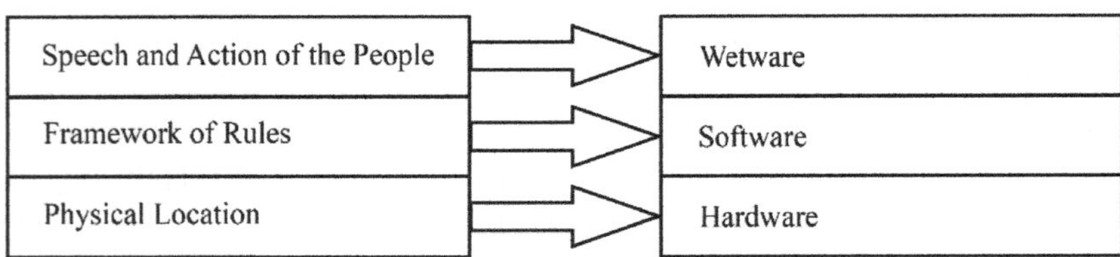

Fig. 1: Three layer structure of the political realm mapped to the three layers of the internet.

activity of people are all necessary. A space with no people cannot be political, just as a people with no place to act politically will not be able to sustain their activity. At the same time, frameworks of rules are required to keep politics bounded and ensure equality and freedom are maintained.

2.4 Hardware, Software, Wetware

Extending the three-layer model of the political realm to the internet can create a more robust model of the online political realm that can enable it to be treated more seriously by demonstrating how it is directly analogous to pre-internet political realms. The physical space, or as Arendt called it, the 'walls' of the *polis*, that simply provide the physical location for people to gather in common is equivalent to the physical infrastructure of the internet. Similar to pre-internet conceptions of the political realm, the fibre optic cables, switches, and routers that form the physical hardware layer of the internet no more determine whether the internet can be a political realm than the walls of the ancient *polis*. The second layer of the constitution or framework of rules and boundaries is equivalent to the software layer of the internet. Like a constitution, the software layer has something of a pre-political character as someone needs to make a website and program how it works before it can become part of the political realm. Software, like constitutions, are rule based mechanisms meant to provide shape to a shared space. The top layer of the pre-internet political realm, namely the people, could in computer terms be called the 'wetware' (Saco 2002, 107). Like in pre-internet space, the people or wetware are clearly the most important element, as politics cannot exist without people and the internet would be uninteresting if no one used it. While each layer depends on the one below it, the entire structure is determined by the people at the top who rely on the lower layers merely to collect themselves into a common space so that they can engage with each other politically. Thus as Barney points out, when Arendt describes the *polis* as not a physical location but as the space between people living together for the purpose of political speech and action, she could have been describing the world wide web (Barney 2003, 108).

By pointing to the online political realm as having the same three-layer model as pre-internet conceptions of the political realm, anti-political arguments which take the guise of being arguments against the technology of the internet can easily be unmasked. Evgeny Morozov for instance, makes the argument that people mostly use the internet for thoroughly non-political purposes and spend most of their time online looking at pictures of cats or pornography, and that therefore the internet as a whole is not suitable for politics (Morozov 2011, 57). Morozov completely discounts the possibility of organizing street protests online like we saw in the Arab Spring because he sees the internet as a space hopeless lost to trivial pursuits and calls any instance of successful activism organized online 'accidental, a statistical certainty rather than a genuine achievement' (Morozov 2011, 180). He goes on to argue that internet use by activists in the Arab world would actually prevent anything from the Arab Spring from occurring, as online organizing is mere entertainment that serves to distract (Morozov 2011, 202–203). Morozov does not merely counsel us to temper our enthusiasm for integrating the internet into politics, but directly argues that doing so will diminish the capacity for politics altogether.

Elisabeth Chaves argues that due to the potential for state or corporate abuse at the hardware layer of DNS routing, the internet cannot serve as a political realm (Chaves 2010, 31–34). She makes the mistake of attributing existing political configurations of internet backbone management to the very essence of the technology. Such arguments come across as inherently defeatist, as few would argue that because offline space is generally configured in anti-political ways we should abandon the terrain altogether. Creating alternatives to the status quo requires vision of what could be, rather than simply evaluating what is and concluding that the status quo is not what we want it to be. A similar argument is made by Robert McChesney who also conflates the hardware and software layers, leading to the argument that the pervasiveness of advertising online makes the internet a problematic space for political engagement (McChesney 2013, 102). The fact that most websites are commercial in purpose simply mirrors the fact that today almost all offline space is commercial and filled with advertisements. While these are problems to be aware of and potential sites for online activism, the same is true for any type of activism. Was occupying Wall Street simply an endorsement of financial capital when activists enter their space to protest? Is marching on public streets paid for by the government in order to protest that same government an inherent contradiction that compromises or co-opts such a protest? We live in a capitalist society, and thus any protest or oppositional politics will inherently be within the terms and confines of capitalism, both online and offline. If a new form of politics is going to arise, it must be out of the status quo, which is an argument that need not be even presented when speaking of offline activism.

The top and middle layers which mark a space as political and provide the framework for a political realm cannot be reduced to the physical layer without rigidifying structures to the point where a protest or any other political act out of the ordinary would be disqualified as political in the first place. What matters when considering the internet is really the nature of web sites and how people use them, as in the pre-internet political realm, the physical aspect is simply there. The internet without the software layer of the world wide web, email, or online games would be an extremely dull place, as its vitality is derived from what people do with it. The malleability of the software layer is what gives the world wide web one of its primary advantages for creating an online political realm. The pre-internet political realms have a tendency to make the software layer of frameworks, constitutions, and informal rules invisible to the point where they get identified with and reduced to the hardware layer, thus giving the appearance that such rules and frameworks are literally set in stone, as politics is associated with the physical structures of the hardware layer, such as a parliament building.

On the internet, web sites are more transparently malleable, especially to anyone with a basic knowledge of computer programming. They were created by people and can be easily changed by people. Lawrence Lessig argues that software code is the law of cyberspace and that its constitutional architecture is continually being built by software developers (Lessig 2006, 6). As Lessig goes on to argue, websites are not simply found and assumed to have rules written in stone in the manner of an offline constitution, but the software design is much more transparently a choice made by people, which can be easily changed or rewritten entirely to create a new set of code which regulates a new website. When a website serves as the middle layer of a framework for the political realm, politics can take on a more dynamic character. It could then be more apparent that politics consists of the actions and relationships formed by those in the political realm, rather than confusing politics with the space it takes place in.

2.5 Immortality and the Political Realm

The two base layers, which consist of a location and a framework of rules for conducting politics, are not political in themselves but attempt to provide some stability, commonality, and permanence to the realm of the political. Since the web of relations established by collective action that constitutes the reality of the political realm is often temporary and transitory, these two lower layers can help make politics more permanent and its effects more durable. As a space of appearance where people can distinguish and reveal who they really are, the political realm serves as a space where people cannot only be recognized in their lifetime but into the future as well. The publicness of the political realm was meant to protect against the futility of individual life in which one simply lives and dies without the ability to leave some lasting trace of one's existence on the world (Arendt 1998, 56). The desire to leave behind a trace of one's life amounts to an attempt to manufacture some degree of immortality, which was to be guaranteed by the permanence of the collective memory of the public realm. The political realm is the means by which people can satisfy the desire to have their uniqueness recognized by others and to leave some lasting trace on the world, things which are extremely difficult away from the presence of others. By creating a permanent and durable public space for politics, political speech and action would become deeds which affected everyone's common existence, and thus become real, memorable, and lasting.

Given the intangibility of political action and the web of relations they form which constitute the most important layer of the political realm, there has been a tendency for political spaces to be transitory, prompting the question of durability. Temporary political spaces, such as Tahrir Square or Zuccotti Park, tend to pop up sporadically but then fade out just as surprisingly as they came into existence. The outburst of political power that overthrew the Egyptian dictator in 2011 and generated intense spaces of politics both online and out in the street already seem to be actions from a distant time as an election resulted in a win for Islamists who were subsequently removed by the military. The same sort of fading of political energy occurred near the end of the surge of protests from 1999 to 2001 surrounding the issue of the globalization of neoliberal economics. While the protests in various cities around the world against the World Trade Organization (WTO) and the International Monetary Fund (IMF) generated intense but temporary political realms, they eventually lost their energy as activists tried and failed to conceive of ways to transform their activism from a situation of transitive reaction to one of more permanent pro-action.

These problems of how to transform vibrant but temporary political spaces into something more lasting are not new, as they have been problems for every outbreak of oppositional politics and every revolution throughout history. According to Arendt, the goal of revolution is to establish a new constitution which provides a lasting framework for how politics is to be conducted. The problem is that there is a tendency in the establishment of new constitutional orders to throw out any kind of concept of a positive right to politics in favour of a framework of negative liberties which ends up reducing politics to parliamentary democracy, thus destroying its radical capabilities. As some critics have argued, this reversion to minimally political parliamentary democracy is the inevitable outcome of Arendt's constitutionalism, even if she herself found parliamentary democracy problematic (Hewlett 2010, 49). This lack of political space open to the people was the fundamental problem of the American constitution which Arendt otherwise admired and which continues to be a problem in countries such as Egypt where an old regime was overthrown and replaced with another form of governance which still negated the political space of the people which had circulated during the revolution (Arendt 2006b, 230).

In contrast to Arendt, for Rancière the tension between the political realm as a contingent construction of the people and the necessity of permanence to give political action lasting effect and continuity is less of a problem. Rancière essentially agrees with Arendt's argument about the political need for a world based on common sense which emphasizes a shared appearance and visibility, but differs in terms of the temporality of political space. In Rancière's view, politics primarily concerns attempts to rearrange and redistribute this sensible world, thus making politics inherently aesthetic (Rancière 2009a, 25). In terms of the political realm, what Rancière is saying is that politics is primarily concerned with rearranging and disrupting established spaces, and, as such, politics takes on a character of continuous aesthetic reordering and, therefore, tends to have a reactive character. Politics is like remodelling a house, and involves moving furniture around and even tearing down walls and adding additions, but in Rancière's analysis, the house is always owned by the anti-political established order, and the political activists doing the remodelling are akin to renters acting without the landlord's permission. The Arendtian question of how to create political spaces that are not simply a matter of rearranging the master's house but which actually carve out a piece of that house to establish a newly ordered permanent political realm is one which Rancière is not interested in, and this is a major weakness; the same weakness that has plagued political activists and revolutionaries alike for centuries.

While I share Rancière's scepticism of transformative utopian projects which only seek to eliminate politics by positing the end of all conflict and disagreement, there is no reason to be similarly sceptical of attempts to establish a more permanent common space which is understood as political and can be a focal point for dissensus rather than utopian forms of consensus. While the WTO and IMF protests of 1999 to 2001 certainly carved out political spaces in a Rancièrian manner by transforming international meetings of technocrats into a space of dissensus and disagreement, these activists eventually burned out on the model of chasing around international finance meetings and, unable to find a focal point for their newly activated political energies at home, the movement itself faded away. While these activists certainly had other and wider interests outside of opposing the WTO or IMF, they had trouble finding a place for their activism outside of the temporary spaces of protest. The question was constantly asked within activist circles of how to carry over the momentum and energy generated during a protest into an ongoing movement for political change. After activists travelled home from a site of protest, whether it was Seattle in 1999 or Quebec City in 2001, there was a sense of frustration due to the lack of outlet to exercise their political energies.

Viewing the political realm as a transitory and temporary phenomenon which occasionally and spontaneously arises to effect a redistribution of the sensible is fundamentally unsatisfying, even if it does result in positive changes. The protests in Seattle were successful in that they transformed the WTO from an obscure international organization into a matter of public debate and arguably pushed later developments in which the WTO became more sensitive to environmental and ethical concerns (Weinstein and Charnovitz 2001). The protests in Quebec City against the Free Trade Area of the Americas were successful in raising vast public awareness and certainly contributed to the agreement being scrapped. Yet even as these movements had a measure of success in bringing change, they still suffered from what Arendt calls the 'lost treasure of revolutionary periods', in which activists became empowered as individuals by participating in intense political activity only to later become melancholic once the space for politics had faded away (Arendt 2006a, 4). There is a feeling that something profound is lost when temporary sites of politics disappear. In critiquing Rancière's definition of politics as redistribution and rearranging without transcending the given order, Žižek argues that he remains within Lacan's discourse of the hysteric. While the hysteric is constantly questioning and challenging the authority of the master, and thus is politically subversive, the hysteric remains within the limits of the master's authority and does not actually seek to transcend that authority (Žižek 2008a, 286). Hewlett levels a similar critique at Rancière, arguing that since Rancière sees politics as always a reaction against the status quo, the failure of radical politics is built into its very definition and no sustained political democracy is possible (Hewlett 2010, 105–111).

Herein lays the paradox of the political realm: as a creation of the energy and vitality of people engaging in politics it tends to be temporary, as attempting to solidify this produced space into something more permanent has a tendency to ossify it into an empty institution devoid of the energy of the people. The bottom two layers of an actual place and constitution become what people call politics, and consequently the action of the people is lost. So either we can accept Rancière's argument that the anti-political police logic is the dominant norm, and politics is an exceptional occurrence of dissensus which generates temporary heterotopias of alternate orderings which then lead to rearrangements of policed space, or we can embrace the circular paradox and try to establish some sort of political realm which has the character of institutional permanence while being fully aware of the tendency for the bottom two layers to constrict and drain away the energy of the people.

While there is no way to resolve the paradox completely, as permanent space will always tend to ossify and become rigid as political energies cannot always be maintained, viewing new political spaces as always open to contestation can be useful in dealing with the paradox. We should aim to create political space with a lasting permanence but also be open to the fact that this political space is not final and may very well depoliticize, necessitating constant re-orderings and redistributions. While the walls of the *polis* did not define Athenian politics, they did help the Athenians who were the content of politics know where to go to be political. To avoid the problem of these walls getting thicker and thicker with time, the boundlessness of political action should be emphasized, along with a self-reflexive attitude in which the boundaries of political space are just as much a matter of political dispute as other non-boundary related issues that are usually deemed to be the content of politics. A more permanent political realm must always be subject to Rancièrian dissensus and reordering in order to stave off the incremental creep of rigidity.

2.6 The Durability and Commonality of a Potential Online World

One of the most important elements of a political realm is its commonality and collective nature. The internet facilitates new forms of communication that mitigate the importance of distance as a practical obstacle to the creation of a common political world. It is on this point that Benjamin Barber's warnings that the internet may have negative effects for politics rely on a fundamental misunderstanding of the nature of the internet. He gives the example of students in one of his lectures who send instant messages back and forth to each other without even looking at each other, despite the fact they are sitting within eyeshot. He argues this is alienating and generates a sense of solitude and loneliness (Barber 2001, 7). In fact, what is happening is the opposite of what Barber thinks: these students are remaining in constant close communication even at a time when they should be paying attention to his lecture, and are thus finding new ways to remain connected. The pervasiveness of online communication has reached a point where the most common popular trope today is no longer about the isolated individual sitting alone in front of a screen cut off from society, but simply social fatigue, as people start to want to have time to themselves where they are not constantly engaged with other people through answering emails, instant messages, Facebook chats, tweets, and text messages. With the early concerns about the internet being isolating and alienating giving way to over-communication, the bigger question is whether all this communication can bring people together to create a durable common political realm or whether it will simply fragment the world into small bubbles of hypercommunication where people no longer feel the need to engage with the larger public because they can establish such pervasive connections within their own social network (Papacharissi 2002, 18).

Bohman argues that the internet is a public of publics with a distributed structure rather than a centralized one, with the implication that it does not matter if there is a single website that everyone goes to for political debate (Bohman 2004, 140). While there certainly can be a multitude of publics, those publics only become a political realm when they come into contact and conflict with each other. In this sense, only temporary political realms could sporadically pop up when different publics came into conflict, but as was argued earlier, there is something wholly unsatisfying about politics as a temporary phenomenon. If the only established place to argue our position and demand change is within a subpublic that we are already a part of and which tends to agree with our position, then such speech is politically useless. The fragmentation of existing political discussion sites into subsites based on a common viewpoint is extremely common and also politically destructive. The ease through which new sites can be created online is a double-edged sword that makes it both easier to create common realms open to all, and to leave the common world and create one's own little realm where no opposing viewpoints can be heard. Due to the malleability of the software layer, the internet can promote both immense commonality and has the potential to create a political realm which actually encompasses the physical Earth, while at the same time can also facilitate fragmentation. As has been emphasized previously, the key is the wetware layer, as people determine how the internet is used, rather than the technology determining what is politically possible.

The malleability of the internet and the importance of human agency remains a tough sell, however, especially on this issue of commonality and fragmentation. Barney argues that the internet destroys the common world of things, built in an Arendtian sense through work, in favour of fleeting consumability (Barney 2003, 110). But the internet is clearly part of this world of things that form the common world and thus are the objects of dispute among those who look at them from different perspectives. The hardware layer of the internet is a literal physical thing, and the software layer enables anyone with even relatively basic computer skills to create a visible object in the form of a website or online posting and to display it publicly. These are tangible objects which can enable commonality around which relationships can be built. The importance of these objects lays in the way that they both bring us together and separate us. Any website that enables political debate does exactly this, as it provides a common forum for everyone to argue their own position in a way that a shopping mall, for instance, does not.

Furthering his attempt to use Arendt to critique the internet's suitability to be a common world, Barney points to Arendt's argument that the fabricated world must be more stable and enduring than the individuals within it, thus guaranteeing that their political deeds will have lasting effect and be remembered (Barney 2003, 112). Barney believes that the internet lacks this durability because of its supposedly fluid and transient nature. While websites certainly come and go, Barney ignores the fact that the internet also enables forms of extreme memory and permanence. Everything online gets copied and backed up as it circulates publicly, making it extremely difficult to get rid of something embarrassing once it gets put online (Rosen 2012). This phenomenon has even spurred a number of recent court rulings where Google has been ordered to remove links to certain material that violates someone's 'right to be forgotten' (Gollom 2014). The internet cannot be both completely consumable and without any memory, and at the same time so extremely permanent that courts have to order the censorship of search results to allow people to hide their past. In fact, one of the ultimate technological fantasies that shows up in everything from Ray Kurzweil's predictions to television shows such as *Caprica* and films such as *Transcendence*, is the ability to harness the data storage and computing capacity of the internet to upload someone's consciousness so they can achieve immortal permanence. Against this background, it is clear that the internet is continuing to grow into a massive collective memory for humanity, and thus can enable the kind of durability a political realm requires in order to ensure that the uniqueness of people's speech and action is remembered.

2.7 The Political Realm as a Space of Appearance

One of the key differences between an Arendtian influenced political realm and a Habermasian influenced public sphere is that the political realm is not merely about the generation of consensus and legitimization but is a space where individuals can reveal themselves as unique subjects. Although Habermas wants to argue against notions of instrumental rationality, his public sphere still has somewhat of an instrumental character in that its purpose is rationalizing the workings of the government through providing a space where the public can develop opinions meant to inform the government, thus leaving them feeling that the government is legitimate in that it listens to their concerns (Habermas 1975, 99–101). In Habermas' account of the public sphere,

> private people come together as a public; they soon claimed the public sphere regulated from above against the public authorities themselves, to engage them in a debate over the general rules' governing relations in the basically privatized but publicly relevant sphere of commodity exchange and social labor (Habermas 1991, 27).

This is similar to Arendt's political realm in that private people come together to publicly use reason to discuss political issues, but by contrast, her political realm has more of a process character in which the performance of politics is an end in itself. In this way, the ability for people to enter the public realm and differentiate themselves from others through political speech and action makes having a political realm necessary in itself, regardless of the outcome of such speech and action.

Politics as a space of appearance is much like the performing arts in that it requires publicity. A theatrical performance witnessed by no one leaves no impact on the world, in the same way as someone giving a political speech which no one hears has no effect. As Arendt notes, what appears in public is not our 'mere bodily existence' as physical objects, but our unique opinions and perspectives (Arendt 1998, 176). While the disclosure of the political subject relates to the world of objects that are held in common, these common objects or political issues form a political realm only insofar as they act as mediators of human action. When an issue such as the distribution of wealth and the influence of financial capital on the government becomes a political issue, such as during the Occupy Wall Street movement, what matters for the creation of a political realm is that these were issues which brought people together (and separated them in disagreement) in political speech and action. It was not the physical location of Zuccotti Park or Wall Street that created the political realm, but instead the actions of the people who shared these places as sites of political concern and contention.

The political realm is a kind of 'in-betweeness' which is intangible but 'no less real than the world of things we visibly have in common' (Arendt 1998, 183). The political realm need not be an actual location where people can literally show their physical bodies, such as a parliament or a protest site, but instead is a web of relations which

> is no less bound to the objective world of things than speech is to the existence of a living body, but the relationship is not like that of a façade or, in Marxian terminology, of an essentially superfluous superstructure affixed to the useful structure of the building itself. (Arendt 1998, 183)

Even though the space of appearance allows us to reveal ourselves in speech and action through the creation of stories, relationships, and changes to the structure of society, the political realm as an intangible connection between people is as real as any other aspect of society. The intangibility of the political realm as a web of relationships means it is not tied to any specific location, and thus the common complaint that protesters need to run for office if they want to engage in politics has no grounding, as clearly a protest can become a temporary political realm in its construction of a web of relationships.

The political realm as a space of appearance can often take on a transitory quality as it comes into being through the speech and action of people and, as a result, can disappear with the dispersal of a people gathered collectively or with the halting of their action (Arendt 1998, 199). In this sense the political realm is a socially produced space in the way described by Henri Lefebvre, as it is only ever the product of human action (Lefebvre 2000). The establishment of official spaces of politics are then no guarantee that politics will in fact occur within those spaces, as is evident by so much of the administrative aspect of modern government which often take on an anti-political quality. Economist Alan S. Blinder is perhaps the most honest representative of this position as he openly argues in favour of depoliticizing parliaments and congresses in favour of more decision making authority for independent technocratic and economically oriented bodies (Blinder 1997). For Blinder the goal is to maintain official political spaces, but then completely strip them of any capacity to do anything political by adopting the model of the independent central bank for more and more aspects of public policy decisions.

The political realm as a space of appearance means it most often takes the form of a disruption, or as a redistribution of the sensible as Rancière puts it (Rancière 2009a, 24). To appear and reveal oneself as a unique subject means that the political realm as a space of appearance is a space 'to render visible what had not been, and to make heard as speakers those who had been perceived as mere noisy animals' (Rancière 2009a, 25). In Rancière's twist on the political as appearance, it becomes a place where people can demonstrate and test their equality, to show not only who they uniquely are by publicly arguing their positions, but to show that they are in fact capable of speaking politically in the first place. Rancière once again provides a useful addition to Arendt's politics of appearance, as Rancière emphasizes the political nature of the attempts of the excluded to appear as political beings in the first place. While Arendt often takes exclusions as a simple fact,[2] Rancière argues that 'politics is about the very existence of a common sphere, the rules of functioning of that sphere, the count of the objects that belong to it and the subjects who are able to deal with it. Politics is about the configuration of the space of politics' (Rancière 2009c, 284). Before one can reveal oneself as an individual and thus distinguish oneself from others by presenting one's unique opinions publicly, one must be able to win the ability to appear and be heard in the first place.

2.8 The Space of Appearance and the Physical Body

What seems to be the biggest problem for postulating the possibility of an online political realm is the issue of appearance. A common argument against online politics is that we cannot really know who we are dealing with, which leads to issues of trust, accountability, legitimacy, and solidarity.[3] This line of argument leads to the question of what exactly appears publicly when one enters the political realm? For a large number of political theorists, including ones drawing on an Arendtian framework, what appears and is revealed in public is the body, and thus the idea of an online political realm is simply a non-starter. Most of these arguments, however, rest on a superficial reading of Arendt which ends up depoliticizing the political realm into a function of the social, a move against which Arendt specifically warned.

In developing a theory of a strong political realm inspired by Arendt, Simon Springer argues that, because political speech and action require public visibility, 'individuals must physically come together to occupy a common space' (Springer 2011, 538). He goes on to argue that the political realm 'is ideally a medium that allows for embodied self-representation' (Springer 2011, 546). He explicitly rules out the possibility of an online political realm, saying it can only function in a Habermasian sense as a communications medium because action in the Arendtian sense requires public visibility, which, according to Springer, means that it must be physically embodied (Springer 2011, 528). The problem with this line of argument is that what is revealed by political action is not the body, as it is not hidden to begin with. Action and opinions, however, need to be revealed because they are not inherently visible, and the manner through which political action is revealed is through the circulation of speech and stories in public. Arendt speaks of the political realm as a web of relations which are generated through action, making it non-material, in that it is not a web of literal physical bodies, but a web of connections, relationships, and stories. A web of physical bodies has no specifically political character to it, and is associated more with the family, cultural, racial, or tribal unit, in which what connects people is literally their bodies. Again, it was the abolition of familial and tribal ties in the reforms of Cleisthenes that brought about democracy in the first place and allowed people to enter a public sphere not as mere physical objects, but as individuals.

Despite this inherently disembodied aspect of the political realm, there is a contemporary unease with the idea of the body as unimportant for politics. Given the relatively recent struggles against exclusions from the public realm because of one's racialized or sexualized body, it can seem as if the body is the very site of politics today. As Andrea Slane points out, the body is also deeply embedded in contemporary notions of democratic citizenship, which rely on the idea of one body granting one vote (Slane 2007, 88). To be a citizen today is not to be a political actor or participant, but to be an officially recognized body within a given geographical boundary. The fact that citizenship is determined not by political participation but by being a body within a given space unnecessarily elevates the body in political importance. The entire premise of representative government also relies on the idea of political space as a collection of bodies in an exclusive space. Arguments about the need for representation are usually premised on the idea that we cannot fit everyone's bodies into one political space, and thus we must send a select few to perform politics on the behalf of the rest.

What the contemporary importance of the body points to is the inversion of public and private that happens in the social realm, which is today the governing norm. The vast body of literature on biopolitics and the associated management of populations and bodies in given spaces are expressions of an anti-political thrust meant to lock people into their bodies as discriminatory and classificatory identities, thus disqualifying people from the political realm on account of the body. As I will argue in the next chapter, what a properly political form of subjectivity seeks to do is disidentify the body as a means of political (dis)qualification. Thus when Mary Dietz writes that Arendt's concept of action is the 'collective power of embodied persons made political', she is positing the appearance of the body publicly as political, when this is the entire argument Arendt makes against the social as being destructive of politics (Dietz 1994, 249). While Dietz is arguing that Arendt is not the anti-feminist she has been made out to be because she argues for a non-gendered political realm, Arendt's argument is not that bodies of any gender can appear politically but rather that bodies are not what appear politically and thus the political realm is not gendered because it has no interest in bodies. As Diana Saco points out, contrary to Dietz's reading, Arendt explicitly opposes identity politics in favour of a public of 'whos' and not 'whats', and that too much emphasis on the body simply generates points of exclusion and discrimination, especially for people with bodily disabilities or those in minority positions (Saco 2002, 56).

What really matters for the political realm in terms of appearing and visibility is the ability to make one's opinions heard and for collective actions to have lasting impact. The presence of the body is not necessary for any of this, as what distinguishes us from others politically is not our bodies or faces, but our words and deeds, along with the stories created by the actions in which we engage (Honig 1993, 80). What matters for the construction of a political realm which allows us to appear is how well it is able to publicize speech and action in order for the uniqueness of individual subjects to be widely recognized. The arguments and opinions of individual people can more easily circulate in writing than in literal speech, and as such, an online space that serves as a political realm can enable more people to participate in a meaningful way that allows their opinions and ideas to become visible. By contrast, to speak audibly with others drastically limits one's potential audience based not just on geography and time, but also based on who might actually be willing to listen. By untying political speech from bodies, the political realm has the potential to radically expand its scope in the same way that the printing press extended the potential readership of literature.

The arguments in favour of embodied political action would have to go so far as to discount any form of written communication as non-political, thus banishing not only the bulk of political theory from having any actual political relevance but also excluding the long history of political pamphleteering as non-political. If political action must be embodied, then the scope of political communication is drastically narrowed to the point where any claims to publicity tend to be lost as embodied speech and action can only reach a very limited audience without some sort of technological extension that would inherently disembody the actors. In this way, even offline political realms are never truly embodied unless they consist of only a handful of people who have no interest in communicating publicly. A political realm which is not public, however, is no longer political if it cannot serve as a space of appearance, equality, and freedom. As was argued previously, politics cannot take place in isolation without turning into the anti-political exercise of coercive force.

A second line of argument against the internet as a space where people can appear politically has less to do with bodies and instead makes an argument that the internet lacks publicity. Brook and Broal claim that computer-mediated interactions are less rich and then go on to argue that they lack the required collectivity and publicity to be political since using the internet places an individual alone in front of a screen (Brook and Boal 1995). The idea that one can be alone while interacting with others seems like an odd claim, and it is doubtful they would make this same claim with regard to talking on the telephone, which could also be claimed to be simply sitting alone with a piece of plastic held to one's head. Such claims expose a deeper problem where people unexperienced with online communications think that they are alone and thus ignore the impact of their actions on the other people they are interacting with. Just because we are not in the physical presence of others when using a computer, does not mean we are alone, as the ability to connect and interact with others is the driving force behind the popularity of the internet.

What Brook and Broal continually allude to in their arguments is their belief that face-to-face communication is simply superior to computer mediated communication. This belief is a common prejudice among critics of the internet. Darin Barney, for example, argues that the internet is private in nature as it allows people to hide and obscure their identity while still being able to interact socially, thus giving it an anti-political character, because no one ever has to reveal who they truly are (Barney 2003, 112). Chris Gray argues that online communication is frankly unsettling and even upsetting because of the lack of awareness of who the other person 'really is' (Gray 2001, 132–133). There is an assumption at work that either the face defines exactly who we are and without its visibility we are nothing, or that what we reveal ourselves to be online simply cannot be trusted. Other than the fairly obvious counter argument that clearly we can know more about who someone like Nietzsche was by reading his books than by looking at pictures of his face, there is a fundamental lack of understanding of how political communication functions at play in these claims.

As James Bohman argues, the claims to the superiority of face to face communication rely on the presumption that political interaction is one to one (Bohman 2004, 133). To talk face to face with someone is to engage in a conversation with at best a few other people, but the entire point of a political realm as public is to enable such speech to reach a wide audience so that one's uniqueness can appear to all. Face to face is probably a superior means of *social* interaction, as when one is interacting with a friend, family member, or love interest, facial expressions and visual cues can be extremely helpful. None of these cues, however, are relevant to political communication, which is by its nature many to many rather than one to one. As Bohman goes on to point out, political speech is always directed at an indefinite and even anonymous audience simply called the public, which expects a response from any or many random persons in that public (Bohman 2004, 134). Politics prior to the internet was never face to face in the first place, and has always relied on some form of technological innovation to transmit speech from one to many and many to one, whether it was the natural architecture of the Pnyx hill in Athens that served as an amphitheatre to carry the speech of one to the many, or the bullhorn or the printing press. The key innovation of the internet is that it not only serves as an artificial means to augment speech but can also serve as the infrastructure for a version of the political realm which can drastically enhance the potential visibility of speech and action by providing a common space that is much less exclusive and more publicly available than offline equivalents such as a parliament or even a protest.

2.9 Ironipolitics and the Internet as Serious Space

Given that when we interact online our bodies are usually not immediately visible, online space is a new experience of interaction which does mark it as different from traditional forms of offline space. It is on this register that the internet often troubles people as its difference can be seen as either threatening or as a new target for anti-political attitudes that can win favour when it seems like the argument against politics is aimed at a new technology instead of the concept of a political realm itself. It is on this issue that many critics of the potential of online political space are eager to point out that online activities are either less real, not serious enough, or fundamentally disconnected from offline political space to have any serious political potential (Morozov 2011). Salvatore, for instance, speaks of activists in Egypt moving from online organization to the 'real world,' as if the internet is some sort of lucid solipsistic dream where nothing is real and that the other people we interact with are simply imaginary (Salvatore 2013, 222). The distinction between physical and virtual is not to be confused with a distinction between real and fake, as we would not claim that our bodies are real while our minds are fake. Just as an offline political realm has three layers and cannot be reduced to its physical elements of walls or borders, online political space comes about from the interactions of people and cannot be reduced to the physical hardware and moving bits which constitute the physical infrastructure of the internet (Saco 2002, 26–27).

The attempt to cast online space as disconnected, unreal, or not serious is an explicitly anti-political spatial strategy that has more to do with opposing politics than critiquing new forms of technology. Drawing on Rancière's typology of anti-political regimes, the attempts to devalue the seriousness of politics by demanding that it be approached with ironic distance could form a fourth type of anti-political regime, which I will label 'ironipolitics'.[4] Ironipolitics is rooted in the belief that the attempt to politically implement grand ideological visions or narratives (such as establishing a political realm) leads to totalitarian cruelty. Thus any political engagements must be primarily grounded in an ethical concern for the difference of the Other, which results in a kind of relativism in which one's own beliefs are not to be taken too seriously for fear they might instigate a conflict with another's beliefs, setting up the possibility for a political disagreement or dispute. Such political disagreements are seen as problematic because decisions may favour one side over another, and thus instigate a totalitarian elimination of difference.

One of the primary theorists of ironipolitics is Richard Rorty, whose underlying concern is avoiding a repeat of totalitarian cruelty, which he views as stemming from too much politics, rather than from the radical negation of politics which it actually was. Rorty proposes a privatization of self-creation which amounts to depoliticizing public political space by transferring any desire to self-create collectively and publicly to the private realm. Politics then becomes a matter of irony, something not to be taken seriously, because any attempts to advocate for one's own 'final vocabulary' over someone else's could escalate into a conflict that might generate cruelty and totalitarianism. Rorty advocates a hollowed out public space that amounts to nothing more than a playful musing among private citizens who do not take their own political opinions seriously, thus depoliticizing any public space which could become political (Rorty 1989, 84). As Derek Barker puts it, Rorty's fear of totalitarianism in the rear-view mirror rules out the institutionalization of ideologies such as Stalinist communism and religious fundamentalism, but it equally excludes participatory democracy, a thicker sense of community, and social equality as serious political ideals (Barker 2009, 100). For Rorty, we self-create and live full lives only in the individualistic private sphere, as any kind of collective action in the public sphere ends up looking like a kind of proto-totalitarianism. Put in Arendtian terms, what Rorty is actually up to is fully embracing the social realm's swallowing of the public and private.

For advocates of ironipolitics, politics itself is not a serious activity, and the internet even less so. A common ironipolitical claim is that everyone on the internet is simply pretending to be someone else; therefore the internet is more of a playground than a space for politics (Gray 2001, 133). The internet is viewed as a realm of 'mere appearance' not to be taken too seriously, even though politics is entirely about issues of appearance, from Arendt's arguments about politics as a space where people can reveal themselves to each other as unique individuals, to Rancière's argument that politics is fundamentally about how the sensible is distributed. The ironipolitical attitude in this respect is a rehash of Plato's cave, where political space online (and offline for that matter) is viewed as a realm of false illusions masking the hidden truth.

The argument that the internet is not a serious place for politics would seem to imply the opposite of the ironipolitical attitude in that the implication is that politics is actually serious and thus must be conducted only in serious offline space. This, however, is part of the ironipolitical deferral, which Derrida's concept of democracy to come illustrates. Derrida's 'democracy to come' is what he calls 'a weapon aimed at the enemies of democracy' who use the word democracy to describe the present situation despite it still lacking full equality, freedom, and rights for all (Derrida 2005, 86). Derrida goes on to point out that the 'to come' part of his phrase 'democracy to come' implies that democracy is both a promise and something that will never exist (Derrida 2005, 86). While Derrida means to use this idea of 'democracy to come' as a way of critiquing existing states who call themselves democratic but could certainly do better, it has the effect of providing a critique of political action as well. Existing political struggles must be treated ironically as something that will not actually bring democracy, thus stripping away the passionate attachment that is necessary to drive political action. Under this rubric, the internet cannot usher in a substantial political realm (as it is always to come), and thus the possibility of an online political realm is to be approached ironically.

In an attempt to remedy the ironipolitical attitude that the internet is fake, not serious enough, or that it constitutes a radically disconnected world with no relevance to offline space, Nathan Jurgenson presents the idea of augmented revolution to provide a model of online and offline space as thoroughly interconnected (Jurgenson 2012, 86). While I share Jurgenson's desire to posit online and offline as connected, he still essentially subordinates the online aspect to being merely a supplement to the offline space. While this model might apply to the Arab Spring and Occupy, where the offline actions were most visible while the internet was more of a site of organization and speech, his model fails to account for the specificity of a political movement such as Anonymous which used offline protests merely as an affirmative supplement to their real actions which took place online. Anonymous also provides an interesting example of the conflict between those who wish to treat the internet as a serious political space and engage in political action which extends and asserts equality, and those who wish to view the internet as a kind of radically disconnected playground where what is done online has no offline consequences.

Anonymous began on the message board 4chan and was, at first, thoroughly ironipolitical in its stance toward the internet. The trollish inhabitants of 4chan, all of whom posted under the same username of 'Anonymous,' believed the internet was not a serious place, that it had no connection to the 'real world', and that there were no offline consequences for online actions. As such, they engaged primarily in message board raids, chat room flooding, disruptions of social games and other behaviour which was motivated by their desire for 'lulz' (internet slang for laughs).[5] As part of their general desire to view the internet as a source of amusement, in 2008 a video was posted on 4chan of actor Tom Cruise discussing his love of Scientology. The video was meant only for people within Scientology, and the over the top performance and statements of Cruise ended up as a source of amusement that made the Church of Scientology an object of ridicule, not just on the somewhat obscure 4chan boards but across the internet as more popular and mainstream websites reposted the video after seeing it on 4chan. As a result, Scientology instigated legal action to have the video removed, drawing the ire of 4chan who organized under the banner of their collective username Anonymous. The 4chan users who would become Anonymous initially viewed Scientology's actions as an attempt to infringe not on their political rights but as an attack on their ability to have fun and laugh at people.

As Scientology's legal campaign grew, Anonymous started to take root and organize a response to Scientology. The movement began to take on a more serious political character, as some Anons (the name for a member of Anonymous) encouraged the group to view Scientology's actions as a fundamental attack on online freedom of expression. Anonymous initiated Project Chanology with a video declaring war on Scientology, which was followed up by attacks on the Scientology website, pranks directed toward prominent members, and manipulating Google search results so that the Scientology website would be the top result on searches for 'dangerous cult'. Anonymous, however, did not fully take on a political character until they organized street protests in various cities in the United States, Australia, Canada, and Europe outside of Scientology Churches. As various activists associated with Anonymous attest to in interviews, before the street protests there was still a sense that Anonymous was not really a movement and may not have been more than a few people (Knappenberger 2012). When tens of thousands of people showed up to protests around the world, it was like this was confirmation that Anonymous actually did exist as a real entity.

The interesting thing to note here was that the bridging of offline and online space, which resulted in the politicization of Anonymous and reversal of its ironipolitical stance toward the internet, did not operate in the same way as the other internet-enabled movements. Anonymous essentially showed up offline and confirmed to itself that this was a real movement, then went back online to focus on hacktivism. For the Arab Spring and Occupy, the protests were organized online and then later it became a matter of engaging in political actions offline. After their Scientology protests, Anonymous went on to provide technical support and services to activists in the Arab Spring and Occupy, and engaged in a number of hacking attempts in support of WikiLeaks, the

Palestinians, and various other political causes (Coleman 2014). During the Tunisian uprising for example, Anonymous hacked the webpage of Tunisian Prime Minister Mohamed Ghannouchi and developed software to subvert government censorship (Norton 2012). Anonymous would go on to attempt a denial of service attack on the New York Stock Exchange's servers to coincide with the Occupy Wall Street protests, engage in attacks on websites related to the Israeli military after their heavy handed operations in Gaza in 2012, and even work to expose a police cover up of a rape by football players in Steubenville, Ohio (Norton 2012). What these actions demonstrate is that online political space itself is increasingly becoming more and more a site of political action and not simply a realm where activists can debate issues and organize offline protests as in Jurgenson's augmented revolution model.

After Project Chanology, many Anons embraced Anonymous's newfound interest in serious political matters, while others argued that they were turning their back on fun and that the internet should continue to be treated in an ironipolitical fashion. The ironipolitical faction of Anonymous engaged in a number of hacking operations after 2008 which were meant to be purely for fun, and worked to discredit Anonymous as a political movement. The most high-profile hack was the 2008 defacement of the Epilepsy Foundation's webpage in which a flashing image meant to provoke a seizure replaced the actual webpage. Given the anonymous nature of the movement, this action generated immense amounts of internal strife as those associated with Project Chanology who were attempting to make Anonymous into a hacktivist movement rather than merely high-tech pranksters were strongly opposed to such mean-spirited and counterproductive actions. Given the decentralized and anonymous nature of the movement, however, this pro-political faction had no proper way of distancing itself from this attack or even expelling those who carried it out in the name of Anonymous (Knappenberger 2012). As time has passed and Anonymous has become more active in supporting other protest movements, the number of these troll attacks has dramatically decreased, especially as numerous Anonymous members were arrested and jailed in relation to these actions. The combination of the success of Anonymous's political actions and the realization that even non-serious hacking meant for laughs was landing Anons in jail has led to the decline in the ironipolitical attitude in which the internet is viewed as a radically disconnected non-serious space with no offline consequences. As the internet continues to become less of a novelty, soon ironipolitical dismissals of online space will sound as unreasonable as dismissing a phone call as 'not real life' because it is not embodied or because it is technologically mediated.

2.10 The Social Realm

In arguing what a political realm entails and why it is needed, the implication is that such a realm does not easily or obviously exist. As alluded to with reference to the protest movements, examples of political realms have tended not to be durable or permanent but sporadically and unexpectedly come into being against the normal state of affairs in which there is very little that could be considered a political realm in the sense described above. Arendt has a name for this situation which characterizes life in the modern liberal democratic state: the social realm. In the modern era there is no longer much of a distinction between public and private, and instead we have the realm of the social where public and private 'constantly flow into each other like waves' (Arendt 1998, 33). In the modern social realm, which devours both the political realm and the private realm, there is an inversion effect at play. Everything that was once considered public, such as politics, is now deemed private, and everything which was once considered private is now displayed publicly. The results of this inversion are especially striking when considering the internet, where governments presume they can spy on the private activities of everyone yet call those who publicize government secrets 'traitors' (Turley 2014). The key difference between the public and private realms, as opposed to the social realm, is the status of publicity and privacy. The separation of the two realms means that some things should not be a matter of public discussion and should be kept private, while others, in particular politics, cannot exist privately and require a broad sense of publicity.

In a situation where the social realm has swallowed up the political realm, the possibility for political action as a means to both distinguish oneself, engage with one's equals, and be free, is greatly diminished. The social excludes action in favour of behaviour, which normalizes people and equates individuals with their status, rank, or categorized identity within society (Arendt 1998, 40–41). In the social realm, action becomes a statistical deviation through which large numbers eliminate the meaning and significance of rare deeds. In politics, it is the statistical outliers consisting of great deeds which are most interesting and relevant, whereas in statistical economics such outliers are thrown out as irrelevant in favour of analyzing the everyday behaviour of consumers and taxpayers (Arendt 1998, 42). Especially in the neoliberal era, even elected officials for the most part attempt to avoid any kind of grand acts in favour of the everyday activity of administration where the highest goal is balancing the national budget rather than performing some great deed that will immortalize them.

While usually the focus is on the social realm eroding the political realm, it eats up the private realm as well. In doing so, our private place where we can hide from others, away from the harsh light of the public is taken away, which in turn makes public life shallower (Arendt 1998, 71). This can be seen even with something as trivial as Hollywood celebrities, as when they are constantly filmed by paparazzi their official public appearances seem hollow and uninteresting. The weight of celebrity depends on not being seen, so that public appearances of celebrity are actually more meaningful. This is especially true for politics, as for most people there are times when they simply want to do something else away from their public political commitments. This is the problem of modern politicians who, in the social realm, are not afforded privacy as their private endeavours are often more of a public concern than their actual activities in parliament. We experience the same uneasiness resulting from the social realm online as well. From Edward Snowden's revelations about extensive government spying, we know that there is a possibility that all of our online actions, no matter how private we hope them to be, are being watched. At the same time, we are constantly warned of the dangers of online anonymity which can facilitate everything from illegal criminal activity to abusive trolling. Both of these contradictory aspects of the how online space operate point to it being characteristic of the social realm.

In many ways homelessness is the primary characteristic of the social realm. There is both no place to go that is truly public and political, and yet also no place that is truly hidden from the gaze of the social, especially in the era of the internet in which every mundane detail of our lives is shared on social networks or is the possible object of government spying. As Benhabib notes, the private realm should function as a shelter for the body, so that when we do enter the political realm, our private person, identity, or body are not threatened as a result of our public opinions (Benhabib 1993, 108). This does not mean that in the political realm one must pretend to be neutral or ignore the fact that our private experiences shape our political views, but simply that one's private life and one's body need protection from the public so that one's political opinions do not harm one's private life away from the public realm. In the social realm, private identities are flung into the public and the result has been an influx of identity-based movements which at best argued for inclusion into the social realm and at worse have attempted to exclude other identities from the social whole. In this sense, the rise of depoliticized multiculturalism and xenophobic outbreaks of violence which focus on private cultural, religious, or ethnic identities are both symptoms of the social realm's attack on privacy. The loss of privacy that accompanies the lack of political space in the social realm is nowhere more apparent than on the internet where the problem of the social is becoming more and more evident. While the social realm has become dominant both offline and online, the capacity to create new political spaces is not lost. As the examples from Egypt, Tunisia, and Occupy demonstrate, activists are increasingly turning to the internet to create political realms that have the capacity to resist both the ossification of official state politics and to some extent even the creep of the social realm.

2.11 Social Networks or Political Networks?

During the recent protest movements in North Africa and with the Occupy movement, Facebook and Twitter rose to prominence as websites that were used heavily by activists. In the case of Egypt, a Facebook page called 'We are all Khaled Said' became a key political space which provided people with not only uncensored news but the chance to discuss and debate issues with each other and to make the connections which would translate into concerted street protests which eventually brought down the government. The Facebook page was created by an Egyptian Google executive to honour Khaled Said, who was tortured to death by Egyptian police after he recorded a video which he posted online of Egyptian police pocketing the spoils of a drug bust (Tudoroiu 2014, 352). The internet was crucial for both exposing police corruption and translating this one instance of police brutality into a wider complaint against the regime. Much has been made of the fact that activists were using social networks, so the question arises as to whether or not these social networks, such as Facebook or Twitter, can be the basis of a new form of online political realm. These spaces can be subject to Rancièrian temporary re-orderings, but as a model of a more permanent political space, their primary nature as *social* networks precludes them from being a basis for more permanent forms of online political space (Rancière 2009a, 24–25).

Arendt's depiction of the common world of political space arising from human activity as a 'web of relationships' is interesting in the context of social networks (Arendt 1998, 182–184). Arendt's web of relationships seems to fit nicely with the currently popular social network model which allows people to form links with others and then circulate stories about themselves and others among their connected friends and followers. However, just as politics does not automatically arise any time people live together, the existence of a technological means to create a world wide web of relationships does not mean such a web will be political. In the case of social networks, these are primarily, as the name suggests, social and not political. The difference between social, public, and private is an aspect of Arendt's political theory that continues to retain importance. As pointed to above, debates about the nature of the internet tend to focus on either the internet being too public or too private, as evidenced by debates about whether what one posts on Facebook is public or private and in the debate surrounding government monitoring of online activity. From an Arendtian point of view, these debates miss the point, as the old divide between public and private no longer exists as they have fallen together into the social (Arendt 1998, 33).

The social realm destroys not just political space, but attacks the existence of the private realm as well. The necessity of a private space outside the light of the public is especially important for children, who 'require the security of concealment in order to mature undisturbed' (Arendt 2006a, 185). Social networking sites are precisely social spaces in that they operate in a manner in which the private life process of a person is put in public view. Even with security settings that may prevent public access, most people are not very discriminating when it comes to who they add as 'friends', and thus a site like Facebook takes on a character as less of a private space where friends share, and more of a publicizing of the private. Facebook founder Mark Zuckerberg makes this ideology of the social explicit in his arguments that the world is becoming more 'public' and less private and thus the incremental loss of privacy on Facebook simply matches the public zeitgeist (Kirkpatrick 2010).

Social networking sites can intensify the publication of the private as personal details placed online can then circulate and become unduly public. Dean argues that this form of undue publicity is the 'ideology of technoculture' in that when one signs up for Facebook one knows very well one is handing over a demographic profile which will be used to sell advertising, but one simply does it anyway (Dean 2003, 101). The problem, however, is not with publicity per se, as Dean would have it, but with the social inversions of public and private that people begrudgingly put up with, either as a result of a lack of computer literacy which leads to lax privacy settings, or simply as the price they have to pay in order to be able to connect with friends on sites such as Facebook (Papacharissi 2010). The ideology of social networks operates more along the lines of Arendt's concept of the social, which should not be surrendered as the nature of online interaction but fought in the manner of Anonymous in order to restore privacy and create a political realm. This is a point which Schwarz glosses over in her otherwise excellent Arendtian critique of social networks: despite the problems with social networks, they constitute but one algorithmic form that online interaction can take, and thus finding problems with social networks as a political model does not in any way diminish the capacity to build a political realm online in another form (Schwarz 2014). What is needed is a sorting out of privacy and publicity so that they apply to appropriate activities.

The tendency of the social to destroy both public and private space make online social spaces problematic as models for politics, despite the structure they share with the political web of relationships. Any form of online political space which is going to strive for any sense of permanence must aim to keep the space political and fight off the counter-attack of the social. When a Facebook page is set up for a political purpose, there is an underlying tendency for the space to revert back toward Facebook's original social nature. The people in the group will often add each other as friends, meaning more and more of an overlap can occur between political and social as people begin to use what was intended as a political page, to share personal announcements with the group, which causes a blurring into the social. Such groups then have a tendency to devolve into social communities where a strict group consensus forms and political disagreement is then viewed as a form of anti-social behaviour leading to the space depoliticizing. Contrary to Malcolm Gladwell's assertion that social networking sites do not lead to political activism (a claim he naively made prior to the Arab Spring and Occupy) because they do not enable the strong ties needed to engage in serious politics, the problem with such social networks is that the ties they establish become too personal and, beyond the initial surge of enthusiasm for a political action, fail to establish a lasting political realm because personal connections among friends lack the agonistic element needed to sustain a robust political realm (Gladwell 2010).

While the anti-political tendency toward socializing a political space is particularly problematic on social networking sites such as Facebook where the user's primary reason for visiting is social and not political, the encroachment of the social is problematic in any form of political space. In the relative early days of widespread internet adoption in the mid to late 1990s, public chat room services offered by AOL and Yahoo! provided political rooms where users could discuss political issues. The interesting aspect of these early chat services was that they were unmoderated and uncensored, and simply had broad topics which brought together people with a variety of opinions and backgrounds. When these services became increasingly difficult to use due to unfixed security flaws and outdated technology, many of the users of these political-based rooms switched to other services which were more user-centric. In the case of the Yahoo! political rooms which I frequented, its dissolution as a common space due to technical issues led to people from those rooms creating their own chat and message board sites in which only those whom they had become friends with were invited. The effect of this loss of common political space led to a proliferation of social spaces populated by people who mostly agreed with each other, leaving them with little to discuss politically, thus establishing a community consensus in which political disagreement became labelled as socially disruptive. What this example demonstrates is that while the internet is rife with political possibility precisely because it is so easy to set up new political spaces, there is a serious danger that these spaces become social if they are not common and accessible to all.

The creation of an online political realm must work in the manner in which Arendt described the walls of the Athenian *polis*, they did not determine that a space was political, as that came from the actions of the people, but the walls did indicate a common space where people could go to engage in political action. Dean's critique of online political activity as too dispersed and ultimately as talking with no one listening speaks to this problem of a lack of common political space on the internet, but the fact that such a common space does not currently exist does not mean it cannot exist (Dean 2009). The problem of online social space not being political is not a limitation of technology but is simply a reflection of the predominant model of offline social space not being political either. But unlike with offline space, online space is much easier to create, shape, and grow. Facebook grew as a social space from the scope of one university campus to being completely global in a matter of a few years. While the social network model is problematic because of its social character, new models of online political space must be created and globalized. Instead of a social network which is primarily centred on people's individual profile pages which are then linked to others as friends or followers, a political web model might instead be focused on political issues which would then link people together in discussion, debate, and decision over a given issue. People would follow topics and issues instead of each other, thus making the political web into a subjectifying rather than identifying mechanism.

To evaluate how political a given situation is, the first criterion must be an analysis of how public space is configured. Given that politics always occurs among other people, those who desire to take part politically must have a designated space where they can go to engage with others who seek to act politically as well. This space need not be official, such as a parliament, but instead can arise wherever people gather to act politically, such as at a protest. Within a political realm, freedom and equality are constructed, tested, and exercised. Political freedom and equality are not natural, but only come about through the collective action of people willing to fight for them. By having a collective political realm, individuals can be recognized by others as unique and can be remembered for having performed political acts. When public space fails to serve as a space of free and equal participation accessible to all, then the given situation is less political than it could be. If a political realm does not exist, or is so constrained that hardly anyone has access to it, then the situation is hardly political at all. Anti-politics works to deny the creation of new political spaces, through the ever present push by the police logic to clear away protesters able to carve out even the most marginal political spaces, and through official rules to ensure that official political spaces remain inaccessible to the broader public.

An Arendtian conception of the political realm, with allowances for Rancièrian reorderings, provides a model of a public sphere that sets the stage for people to become political subjects, participate in political debate and decision making, and play out their disagreements and conflicts publicly. By placing the political realm online, the entire structure of representative government can come into question as spaces can be created that negate the need to send a limited number of representatives to a limited physical space. The internet has elements of both extreme publicity and extreme privacy, which mark it as social in character. To fend off the depoliticizing influence of the social, activists must focus on ensuring that the privacy of individuals is protected online, while continuing to push for the creation of political spaces which are open, transparent, and accessible. If space is socially produced, then political space can be produced online. In this manner, an online political realm can be superior to traditional pre-internet conceptions of a political realm because it can be more inclusive and participatory, facilitate more robust forms of political subjectivity, and ease the ability to assert conflict in the form of disagreement and dissent. These three aspects of politics will be dealt with in the following chapters and will provide the content for what happens within the online political realm.

CHAPTER 3

Subjectivity

3.1 Political Subjectivity and the Emptiness of the Universal

The question of subjectivity is inherently linked to the question of the political realm. In order to have a political realm, there must be people who enter that realm for the purpose of engaging in politics. The political subject as an empty universal is significant, as it puts the emphasis on the people as the centre of politics. By conceptualizing the political subject in such a way, it becomes open to all and politics becomes relevant to all. An identity-based movement is only relevant to those within the identity, a citizen-based politics is only relevant to those who hold legal status within a specific state, and a subject based on Enlightenment ideals has too many positive qualifications which have led to unjust exclusions in the past. The political subject as universal means that the subject's speech and action is relevant to all and is addressed to the public, while its emptiness enables plurality, as there are no specific qualifications or positive attributes that someone must have in order to become a subject. Such a conception of the political subject is especially interesting in an online political realm where bodies, identities, and status qualifications tend to be obscured, making online political interactions naturally suited to an empty universal form of the political subject.

On the surface, there are similarities between the theory of the political subject I will advance here and the Enlightenment liberal subject, or simply the citizen, on account of the emphasis on the universality of political subjectivity. The alleged universality of the modern liberal subject, however, has come under attack from all quarters. As Vincent Descombes argues, an attack on the illusion of subjectivity seemed to have been the primary preoccupation of French philosophy in the second half of the twentieth century, with both poststructuralists and Heideggerians seeking to banish the spectre of Enlightenment subjectivity (Descombes 1988, 123–124). Feminism has pointed out that

---

How to cite this book chapter:

Smith, T. G. 2017. *Politicizing Digital Space: Theory, The Internet, and Renewing Democracy.* Pp. 41–69. London: University of Westminster Press. DOI: https://doi.org/10.16997/book5.c. License: CC-BY-NC-ND 4.0

the modern liberal political subject was assumed to be a male, postcolonial studies has taught us that this subject also was assumed to be white, and queer studies points out that it was assumed to be heterosexual as well. The modern liberal subject has been widely exposed as not universal but instead as a particular identity which has attempted to elevate its particularity to a hegemonic status through imperial impositions.

These are all valid critiques, but the reaction to the false universality of the modern liberal subject has been to assert a plethora of particularities against it and emphasize difference over universal equality (Nicholson and Seidman 1995). Political subjectivity is thrown out in favour of multiple or shifting identities which assert their own particularity against another particularity which falsely claims to be universal. If, however, the universality of the modern subject is exposed to be nothing more than one particularity attempting to impose itself on all others, and is to be rejected as its various critics argue, the assertion of other particularities is not a proper solution. As Sergei Prozorov points out, 'is not the problem with universalism precisely that the allegedly universal was *in fact* particular' (Prozorov 2014, xvii)? The proliferation of identity politics, multiculturalism, and poststructuralist theories of shifting and multiple identity are not a solution to the problem of the false universalism of the modern liberal subject because they fail to solve the problem of fake universalism that they rightfully questioned in the first place.

The root of the problem with the modern liberal political subject was that it attempted to ground its universality on foundationalist principles. There would be appeals to God, nature, or history as an attempt to justify filling in the universal with a specific particular. Such attempts to ground the political community on solid foundations of an unquestionable and authoritative basis, however, end up destroying plurality as those who do not agree with the grounding principles are simply cast out of politics. As was argued in the previous chapter, the political realm is a human creation that must be built, and thus it has no natural grounding. As Arendt points out with respect to the American Declaration of Independence, Thomas Jefferson perhaps had an inkling of the wholly constructed and contingent nature of the political realm when he wrote 'we hold these truths to be self-evident', a clear contradiction as self-evident truth need not be 'held', which implies the truths of American politics are actually a human construction (Arendt 2006b, 185). In this sense, what holds the political realm together is not that the individual subjects have rationally come together to decide that based on a set of natural truths this is the way the community must be governed, but instead through a recognition that the universal is groundless and therefore empty.

The universality of the political subject stems from its emptiness, or, what we have in common is *nothing*. Unlike the theorists of consensus or particularized identity who argue that conflict leads to violence or totalitarian erasures of difference, having nothing in common does not eliminate the potential for politics, but instead calls it into existence. In an Arendtian sense, we build the common world simply to give ourselves an agonistic space to test out our subjective opinions against those of others and to provide a political means to decide common matters which have no objective answers. A politics which embraces the ability for each to try to persuade the rest is a direct substitute for violent force, which imposes a single solution from above. If the common world demanded the commonality of subjects, then universality would be impossible precisely because to be the same as others demands that difference be excluded and subjective plurality be erased. The Occupy movement serves as an excellent example of such empty universal subjectivity as it could not be reduced to a singular identity or situation, and thus was able to manifest itself in over 100 different countries.

Becoming a political subject means elevating oneself out of the particulars of identity and into the realm of universal concern, where one can express one's own opinion and respond to others, marking one as a unique individual. Particular identities are what make us like everyone else, in that to be identified as a Muslim, Korean, or lesbian is to be placed and categorized as not a unique individual but as part of a general group where all members have the same properties. Political subjectivity moves outside of these identity categories in that the political subject reveals him or herself to be someone unique who is part of that unidentifiable part of society which commonly takes the name of 'the people'. The logic of the anti-political state is one of identification, in which there can be no empty universal position that floats above the hierarchy of ordered and identified parts and thus no critical debate about issues that affect everyone. Subjectivity is an important terrain of contestation between politics and anti-politics as the identification mechanism of keeping everyone in their assigned place is an attempt to foreclose the emergence of political subjects and shut down the possibility of politics itself.

3.2 The Withdrawal from Identity

Against the recent push to do away with the political subject altogether, exemplified by 1991's *Who Comes After the Subject* (Cadava, Connor, and Nancy 1991), there has been a drive to reassert the importance of political subjectivity in its universal form by a group of contemporary theorists ranging from those who took their starting point with Althusser (Rancière, Badiou, and Balibar), to others more influenced by Lacanian psychoanalysis (Žižek, Zupančič, Mouffe and Laclau). In his *Metapolitics* (2011, 58–66), Badiou argues that Althusser began to think a 'subjectivity without a subject' which Badiou positions as one of two of Althusser's major contributions to political theory. Badiou states that Althusser's attempts to build a theory of the subject have recently been 'carried out with an international zeal' (2011, 58). Included in this research is of course Rancière, who has positioned himself against Althusser since the publication of his *Althusser's Lesson* in 1974. Badiou also bridges over to the Lacanian position on political subjectivity, as he along with Žižek and Mouffe have connected the subject's emptiness with the psychoanalytic concept of lack (Stavrakakis 2007, 40). While Arendt had no engagement with Althusser and certainly had little interest in psychoanalysis, her focus on free and equal subjects striving for immortality within a political realm which functions as a universal world without positive properties puts her thinking in line with many of these thinkers, despite their often harsh critiques of her thought.

A common source among these contemporary theorists of the empty universal is Hegel, and in particular Alexandre Kojève's interpretation of Hegel which revitalized French philosophy after the First World War. In Kojève's interpretation, the Hegelian subject is driven by the desire to be recognized by others. Desire implies the presence of an absence in the form of a lack, which leads the human subject to 'negate given being' and thus attempt to change the world in an attempt to satisfy the desire that is driven by the lack, which is a lack of recognition (Kojève 1980, 38). Action in a political sense has a negative and subtractive character before it can have a bigger political impact. If one is simply satisfied with what is, then one does not act. Since the goal of these actions is recognition, political subjectivity is necessarily universal, as to be recognized by one person or even a thousand people is not satisfying if one can still face the discrimination and disempowerment of a lack of recognition from others. Now Arendt is not a Hegelian, but she explains the function of political subjectivity in much the same way. She argues that what drives people to enter the political realm and become political subjects is the desire to leave some lasting trace on the world, and thus achieve a form of immortality. The great performative deeds of speech and action which characterize politics can achieve immortality for the subject only in so far as these deeds become universally known, leading the subject-actor to become universally recognized.

In order to be able to distinguish oneself amongst one's equals in word and deed as Arendt describes, first one must be recognized on a basic level as an equal capable of engaging in political speech in the first place. It is in this sense that Kojève describes recognition as an overcoming of oppression. For Rancière, it is this kind of striving to overcome wrong that drives people toward political subjectivation, rather than an Arendtian sense of striving to leave a trace and be remembered (Rancière 1999, 39). When one realizes there is something wrong in the world, it motivates one to act, which requires that one must first step out of one's assigned place and role within society. This means taking a risk to try to enact a change in the world which brings about more equality. The political subjectivation process that seeks to bring about freedom and equality in the Rancièrian sense is then a necessary prerequisite to acting as a subject in the Arendtian sense, although the two forms of subjectivation are usually linked, as correcting a wrong brings about a universal change in the world, thus winning the actors immortal fame in the process. Both of these motivations to become a political subject based on recognition act as a corrective to Kojève's belief that once everyone was universally recognized, and thus free and equal, there would be no more politics. Even if it were possible to purge all positive identifications and (dis)qualifications from the political realm, something which is likely impossible, there would still be the action of equals striving to distinguish themselves which would drive people to enter the political realm.

Taking his starting point from Kojève's claim that all political action begins with negation, in many ways Slavoj Žižek's *The Ticklish Subject* is an interesting synthesis of much of the contemporary political theory which seeks to reassert the importance of the political subject and in particular its universality. Encompassing insights from Rancière, Badiou, Laclau, and Mouffe, as read through his Hegelian-Lacanian perspective, Žižek posits subjectivity as a three step process. First there is a withdrawal from the world, followed by a plunge into madness, eventually allowing an emergence from madness to create a symbolic universe (Žižek 2008a, 36–38). To put this process of subjectivation in political terms, it means that to become a subject one must first withdraw from one's particular place in society, strip away all identification and classification and thus negate given-being in Kojève's terminology, which will then allow one to come back into the shared and universal world of politics. As Žižek puts it,

> you become 'something' (you are counted as a subject) only after going through the zero-point, after being deprived of all the 'pathological' (in the Kantian sense of empirical, contingent) features that support your identity, and thus are reduced to 'nothing'—'a Nothingness counted as Something'(Žižek 2008a, 183).

In other words, to become a political subject, or to reveal oneself as someone with political substance ('something'), one must leave behind the particularities of identity that are used by the anti-political order to categorize, place, count, and ultimately dismiss one as incapable of political speech. By negating one's given-being, or identity-place in the world, and embracing one's lack, one can then emerge to perform acts of universal significance that can both lead to recognition and change the world. If one is satisfied by one's particular place in the world, or one's own identity, one will not have the desire to act politically. The lack that drives the desire to act will be filled, and the goal of such individuals will simply involve replicating the status quo rather than taking the risk to disrupt their own satisfaction and bring about political change.

In virtually every protest movement that arises, there is a concerted attempt by the apparatuses of anti-politics to identify the protesters in order to categorize and dismiss them as simply concerned with their own identity interests with nothing relevant to say to everyone else. In the Arab Spring there were continuous attempts to identity protesters as foreign disrupters who should not be listened to (Fleishman and Richter 2011), and in the context of Occupy the protesters were labelled and dismissed as everything from hostile to America and thus not to be trusted, to disingenuous pawns of the labour movement trying to distract the public from the failings of President Obama (Becker 2011). Such attempts to uncover a hidden particularity are meant to reveal the activists as self-interested parties with nothing to say to the wider public. A prime example would be the 2013 protests in the Canadian province of New Brunswick against exploratory drilling for shale gas, commonly called fracking. While these protests began as a grassroots coalition between environmentalists, people in rural areas concerned about water quality, and aboriginal groups, the media was quick to identify and dismiss the protesters as merely an aboriginal complaint about land use, thus papering over the water safety issue. Such a framing was meant to convince the average Canadian that these protests were of no wider consequence since aboriginals are a small minority and a land claim dispute does not affect the vast majority of Canadians.

The key difference between this idea of subjectivity as a stripping away of particulars and the old Enlightenment political subject of universal reason revolves around the difference between adding and subtracting. Žižek likes to tell a joke to elaborate on his conception of subjectivity about a worker who leaves a factory every day with an empty wheelbarrow who the bosses believe is stealing from them. The bosses check the wheelbarrow every day but cannot figure out what he is stealing because the wheelbarrow is always empty. But Žižek says this is precisely the point of subjectivity, that it is empty, as the worker is stealing the wheelbarrows themselves (Žižek 2008a, 132). This is what the old Enlightenment idea of political subjectivity misses; the fact that subjectivity is empty and without specific properties is exactly what makes it universal, not the ability to rationally come to a consensus on a set of values that must be universally true and agreed on by all. To become a political subject involves emptying our wheelbarrows, not making sure everyone has the same things in their wheelbarrows.

While everyone having nothing can be truly universal, a situation in which everyone's wheelbarrows are filled exactly the same way is virtually impossible. It is also why the anti-political order seems to be disproportionately threatened by protests that advocate not for any one specific identity-cause, but operate in a manner so that anyone can project whatever complaint they have onto the protest and thus join in. The vexation of many commentators about what Occupy really was about relates to this empty universality and the difficulty in trying to categorize, count, and place these people who were making a general argument about corporate greed and government complacency, and not making a specific identity claim about a certain group needing to be given a place within the whole. Identity claims are inherently static, as they seek to keep people in their place, while political subjectivity posits an empty universality free from classification and open to all who are willing to cast aside static placements and move among those who have no place or qualification.

3.3 Political Subjectivity Online

In the previous chapter I argued that a political realm can be created on the internet, as political space was a product of the actions and movements of people and thus not reducible to hardware. The experience of activists in the Arab Spring, Occupy, and Anonymous movements testify to the creation of online political space, which raises the question of online political subjectivity. Does operating in an online political space change, alter, or reorient the political subjectivation process? What I argue is that the act of entering an online political realm, even if it is just a discussion forum for politics, automatically pushes people into the subjectivation process by stripping away their offline identity and throwing them into the universal void of the internet. In this manner, the siting of politics in an online political realm can be a tremendous aid for overcoming the many obstacles that prevent people from activating their own political subjectivity.

If the first step of becoming a political subject is to strip away all forms of contingent particular identity, going online to discuss politics operates in the same manner. Imagine a scenario in which one finds a political discussion site on the internet for the first time. After choosing a username, one joins in a debate by posting one's first comment. This person enters the discussion as someone who is completely unidentifiable and completely without properties that others can recognize. The other people using the site see only a username and the comment that was posted, meaning that the first time user has no identifiable particularities on which to be judged or dismissed. Those who seek to engage with this first time commenter can only respond to what the comment said, as they know nothing of their identity, class, status, or bodily traits such as sex or skin colour. The simple act of going online and entering into a pseudonymous space automatically strips away identities, as your body and social background are invisible to the other commenters as a source of prejudice. The very nature of such online interactions forces a subjectivation process, because nothing is visible except the story that is revealed through our online speech. Online interactions within a website dedicated to political discussion are the ultimate form of Cartesian subjectivity, as what we think and share with others is what defines us to the others, not the sight of our bodies. Political disqualification based on prejudice is radically subverted as there is simply no grounds on which to pre-judge someone and thus disqualify him or her before he or she even has a chance to speak. Attempts to disqualify someone as incapable of political speech in an online context then must always allow for at least some form of initial speech and revealing of subjectivity. By contrast, in offline space one can see someone's body before they ever speak. Offline prejudicial dismissals based on physical appearance can become the grounds for disqualifying someone's political speech before one can even make an initial statement.

Without prejudice to rely on as a means of disqualifying someone from political speech, anti-political mechanisms based on disqualifying speech via identity are disrupted. By hiding these prejudices and protecting private identity through adopting a pseudonym, the anti-political identification process is already rendered less effective. People have already been admitted into the political realm and attempts to dismiss their capacity to speak politically must come after the fact. While pseudonymity may not entirely protect private identities from attacks meant to disqualify one's speech based on identity, as these identities may become apparent in the context of longer discussions or may be purposely revealed by the speaker, at least the effect of prejudice is severely limited. The fact that such attempts at disqualification must come after one has already spoken as a political subject within a political realm marks a significant advantage for online political speech over offline, as identificatory disqualification after one has already entered the political realm as a political subject remain difficult online if one is careful to keep their private identity hidden.

In existing online political forums, one inevitably encounters someone who disagrees with what one says, but has no counter-argument and, instead, tries to shut down the debate by using the anti-political method of attempting to identify, classify, and thus 'put you in your place', a place where one is not qualified to speak politically. Such attempts can be easily frustrated online by refusing to identify one's particular characteristics. The attempt at classificatory dismissal fails, as the person attempting the dismissal does not know where exactly the other's place is and thus does not know how to politically disqualify the other's speech. This works in stark contrast to an in-person political debate, where bodies are visible and prejudices surrounding skin colour, sex, economic class, or cultural identity are much easier to spot and use as classificatory ammunition, either through direct appearance or through some basic research into that person's private background, as public and private personas are usually directly connected in offline politics. The act of going online can be emancipatory in itself, as a person's offline minority status can be obscured, allowing individuals to easily emerge from their minority positions which are used to disqualify them from taking part in offline politics. When one's identity is the source of prejudice, to keep it hidden online makes revealing oneself as a unique individual with unique thoughts and opinions much easier.

Stromer-Galley and Wichowski point to the experience of many women in early political chat rooms who found that not mentioning their sex allowed them to take part in discussions without having to worry about harassment or disparaging comments painting them as unfit to participate (Stromer-Galley and Wichowski 2011, 174). The same authors also found that those who are reluctant to discuss political matters offline, outside of their immediate circle of friends or family, were more willing to engage in political discussion with strangers online (Stromer-Galley and Wichowski 2011, 175). The fact that people have to hide something like their sex, skin colour, or sexual orientation, because they are ammunition for anti-political attempts to disqualify their speech demonstrates the pervasiveness of anti-political attitudes. While simply hiding the point of discrimination will not end discrimination, it does force it to become less personalized to the point of preventing someone from participating in a discussion. The forced subjectivity of pseudonymous interaction can enable a more egalitarian form of political discussion, as most people will simply assume that everyone else is like them, until they are provided proof to the contrary. In this sense, if one goes to the various country-specific Reddit discussion forums with an ambiguous username and simply jumps into the conversation, everyone else will simply assume one is from that country until provided with evidence to the contrary. So long as a user does not volunteer this identity information, there tend to be few discriminatory barriers to entry to such pseudonymous forums.

The erasure of identity that is experienced when entering an online political discussion site does not, of course, mean that we lose our private identities altogether, but only that when speaking politically we speak universally as someone with something to say to the all, rather than as an undifferentiated member of an identity whose concerns are only related to that specific group. By leaving these identifications in the private realm they fail to serve as disqualifiers of political subjectivity. The withdrawal from identity that happens automatically when entering online pseudonymous political spaces is not about full-on eliminating our private identities but as experiencing them as wholly contingent, something which has been the basis of political subjectivity since Cleisthenes. In this sense, revealing one's identity online can be a form of proving that this identity actually has no power to disqualify. When online discussions about racism arise, someone may identify as a member of the target group for the sole purpose of pointing out how that identity is completely contingent, as here they are speaking as a universal subject against forms of racism and discrimination. By speaking as a political subject, it is proven that traditional identities which have been used to disqualify political speech are as irrelevant to political speech as identities or quirks which have not been used to disqualify and identify. Demonstrating the irrelevance of such identities causes them to lose their authority to disqualify, and puts them in the same category as having a private identity as a stamp collector or being left handed: categories which have no relevance to one's ability to speak politically and make universally relevant arguments.

3.4 Madness and Protest

Žižek's argument that the subject's stripping away of identity induces a sort of madness has direct political implications. He argues that the terror and upheaval of revolutions relates to this stripping of previous identities and allows a new order to arise (Žižek 2008a, 108). While revolutions and protests need not relive the terror in the same manner of the French Revolution, they do tend to have similar processes that could be linked to the madness that accompanies a withdrawal of all identity. In particular the black bloc protest technique, which first gained public notoriety in the 1999 Seattle WTO protests and has recently been adapted by Egyptian activists protesting the Muslim Brotherhood government (Rosenfeld 2013), operates as a physical expression of the subjectivizing process of withdrawal and stripping away of identity. In a black bloc, the protesters all wear similar black clothes and masks as a means to obscure their own individual identities and express a kind of collective solidarity with the other protesters. The fact that the black bloc technique is often associated with more aggressive protest methods, such as direct confrontations with police and property damage, mark it as both a stripping of identity and a kind of descent into necessary madness in order to eventually emerge to create a new universal order. In Egypt, black bloc protesters were explicitly stripping themselves of Muslim identity and targeted the offices of the Muslim Brotherhood and Islamist Freedom and Justice Party with arson attacks with the goal of secularizing the government and making it responsive to the people in general, rather than just a certain portion of the people who identify as Muslims.

The protest technique of obscuring identity is an essential aspect of the subjectivation process. To put on a mask is not simply to prevent identification and possible arrest by the police, but is to strip oneself of the particular elements that sustain a private identity which is the object of classification, administration, and policing by the anti-political state and economic system. Laws against concealing identity in a protest and media criticism of protesters as hiding when they wear masks is a deeply anti-political ploy to cut off the subjectivization process at its very beginning. If individuals can remain objects of identification, then their speech can be classified and dismissed as politically irrelevant to the whole, and that threatening universality known as the people, can be prevented from forming. Interesting parallels also arise here with regard to the debate about online anonymity, which put in the context of identity-concealing protests, clearly becomes an issue not of technology but of the difference between political and anti-political approaches.

3.5 The Madness of Disembodied Online Interaction

If the subject-formation process can be likened to a descent into madness before one emerges as a universal subject, then for those who are used to having their particular identities bestow privilege, interacting online can seem like madness. The suspicion that people seem to have toward expressions of identity by others online is an entirely positive trait, as it helps reinforce the egalitarian stripping away of identity, especially when someone proclaims an identity that is meant to mark one as privileged. Even if someone really was a millionaire, no one online will believe the claim, and thus any kind of political argument relying on the authority of class will simply fall flat. To the millionaire who is used to privilege, especially if he or she is also used to privilege in their face to face interactions from not just economic class but from gender and skin colour as well, arguing about politics on the internet would very much seem like pure madness. No one respects his or her identity and privilege claims, forcing the person claiming identity privilege into a form of equality in which his or her thoughts and opinions must stand on their own ground. In this context, the complaints made by some about the loss of identity online as unsettling and problematic expose underlying hostilities to the egalitarian nature of political subjectivity. Gray, for instance, is very insistent that online interactions are creepy and unsettling because he does not know the true identity of who he is talking to and they do not know his true identity. He then concludes that because of this lack of identity, the internet is therefore unsuited for political discussion (Gray 2001, 132). The internet only seems like madness if one's particular identity grants offline privilege, but for an egalitarian politics such madness is politically necessary.

Oddly enough, the uncertainty surrounding the true identity with whom we interact online seems like a problem for Žižek himself. He has commented about the potential for violent objectification of other people when we interact online due to not knowing their true identity (Žižek 2007). If, however, we return to Žižek's wheelbarrow joke, in which the wheelbarrow of subjectivity needs to be emptied of identity before it can be filled up with substantial political content, here we have Žižek claiming that in order to build political solidarity online we need to know what identity was in the wheelbarrow before it was emptied out at the start of the subjectivation process. The problem of treating people like objects and thus invoking the spectre of violence is not some kind of inherent aspect of online interaction, but, as Žižek himself explains outside of the context of the internet, is a result of the anti-political identification process which places people into objective groups to be acted on, which denies their subjective individuality. The act of going online empties our wheelbarrows out for us, making becoming a subject in the Žižekian sense even easier, despite Žižek's own seeming unease with the technology which leads him into contradictory statements.

Similar to Žižek's argument, Turkle claims that interacting online is depersonalizing and therefore degrading (Turkle 2011). Not only is this untrue in general, as each webspace is different, but in a political context depersonalization is beneficial. In any political discussion the goal should be to evaluate the statements and arguments being made on their own merits, independently of the identity of the person making the statements. The idea that the body needs to be visibly present in order to prevent ethical degradation relies on the idea that bodies are not sites of Foucauldian biopower but instead usher in ethical respect. By contrast, identity and the body are most often sites of oppression which are overcome through political speech and action. If the body bestowed ethical status, there would be no debates about the rights of those who are politically disenfranchised, because as pure bodies they should be afforded the highest ethical status according to Turkle's argument. The ethical situation of stateless peoples demonstrates how this argument is problematic, as such people are objects of sovereign authority which reduces them to a status of bare life (Agamben 1998, 126–134). Even more striking is the case of animals, who lacking any sort of ability to transcend their bodies and assert themselves through political speech, are the extreme objects of ethical degradation, demonstrating that a lack of ethical respect resulting in objectification is a huge problem for those who cannot transcend bodily identity.

3.6 Disembodied Online Subjects

While I have argued that stripping away particular identities, especially those rooted in biology, are necessary for the subject-formation process, a line of argument constantly arises when speaking about online interactions that states that because these interactions with other people are not embodied they are therefore not real or at least less valuable or authentic. Face to face communication is claimed to be superior and even necessary for political interaction for a number of rather flimsy reasons which I dealt with in the previous chapter. Many of these arguments in favour of embodied subjectivity begin with the assumption that 'in the physical world there is an inherent unity to the self, for the body provides a compelling and convenient definition of identity. The norm is: one body, one identity' (Donath 1999, 27). The body is then claimed to be a 'stabilizing anchor', and thus when it is obscured online, we can lose our sense of self (Donath 1999, 27). This assumption leads to two camps critical of online disembodiment: on one side are those who accept online subjectivity as disembodied and then go on to argue this disqualifies it from being authentically political, and on the other are those who attempt to salvage the possibility of online politics by claiming that online subjectivity is actually embodied after all. But given that political subjectivization involves subtracting oneself from positive identifications, including those that have been built up around the body (either as something oppressive or as a positive culture) both of these camps fail to properly appreciate how a disembodied and de-identified online experience can be extremely beneficial for the formation of political subjects and the sustainability of an online political realm.

Representative of the critics of online disembodiment are Brook and Boal, who claim that embodied face-to-face interactions 'are inherently richer than mediated interactions' (Brook and Boal 1995). Statements like this are problematic, because not only is it not obvious that such interactions are 'richer,' but there is an implicit claim that embodied interaction is not mediated. Such claims rely on a romanticized idea of social interaction in which looking into someone's eyes during a conversation creates a magical neural link which allows access to the other's true thoughts. In reality all interactions are mediated, and face to face interactions are mediated by social customs, the space in which such interactions take place, as well as the relationship, status, and position of those interacting (Shannon and Weaver 1949). The fact that interaction is mediated is not an issue in itself but how it is mediated. If the interaction is mediated by the fact that one person is of a lower economic class or perceived social status than the other, this can be problematic and cause one person to unnecessarily defer to the other. Mediations like this are politically problematic whether they occur in-person or through a computer. Furthermore, the claim that in-person interaction is richer relies on the presumption of a certain personality type, as those with more extroverted personalities find in person interaction easier, while those with more introverted personalities can have a hard time expressing themselves in person and do better when they are provided with the time to think that is afforded by computer-mediated conversation (Amichai-Hamburger, Wainapel, and Fox 2002). For many people, computer mediated interaction feels richer because it is easier to communicate, especially for those with physical disabilities (Bowker and Tuffin 2002), demonstrating that claims about an 'inherent richness' to face to face interaction, especially when speaking of political interaction, rely on a set of anti-technological and personality type biases.

A further critique of disembodied interaction comes from Gray who claims that, because citizenship is based on bodies within geographical boundaries, to be disembodied is to not be a citizen and thus have no stake in politics (Gray 2001, 29). Gray's statement that citizenship is embodied simply demonstrates how citizenship has been depoliticized into a matter of where one is born, rather than as a matter of taking part in politics. The goal of political subjectivation is precisely to make one into more than one's body in order to allow one's unique individuality to shine through, something that has nothing to do with birth or naturalization-based citizenship. Gray would also go so far as to disqualify the hacktivism of movements like Anonymous as thoroughly non-political because they are not embodied (Gray 2001, 44). By this same line of reasoning, politics cannot be conducted over the phone and the entire concept of representative government that Gray is a strong advocate of, is illegitimate because it rests on the presumption that a person's opinions can be separated from their physical bodies and represented by someone else.

The key to understanding online disembodied subjectivity is that when we use the internet to discuss politics, we are primarily interacting with other people and not with a computer, smartphone, or other web-enabled device. Critics of the idea of online disembodiment, such as Paul Dourish, make the mistake of extrapolating embodied interaction with the physical objects of technology to social relations themselves (Dourish 2004, 18–19). For human computer interaction researchers, such as Dourish, the embodied relation with our interface device is of prime importance, but the fact that we use a mouse or a keyboard to discuss politics with others online does not make those interactions embodied. The embodied relation with the computer takes place in the private sphere outside, and before, what is happening on the screen (Saco 2002, 133). In the context of a political discussion site, others experience our own subjectivity as thoroughly disembodied, as all that is presented is a username and written thoughts. The fact that we use our bodies to type on a keyboard while sitting in front of a computer or thumb at a mobile phone while walking down the street does not make the relation between those who are participating in the online political discussion embodied.

While anyone who has been bumped into by someone walking down the street with their head down, completely absorbed in what he or she is doing on their phone can attest to how mobile computing devices are doing anything but increasing embodied presence, Jason Farman makes the argument that such devices enable an interface between virtual and physical spaces which does in fact promote embodiment (Farman 2011). While much of Farman's analysis of mobile interfaces is interesting, he draws the wrong conclusion, in that such devices enhance our ability to escape the body. The panic of being lost is an example of pure embodiment, as our mental map of where we are fails and we are forced to rely on immediate physical surroundings which are unfamiliar. The ability to pull out a phone with GPS and see where we are does not increase our embodiment in physical space but enhances our disembodied sense of where we are and where we are going on our abstract mental map, which can be represented as the little dot that shows our exact location on a map displayed on a phone.

Politically speaking, the heavy use of mobile phones during the revolutions in Tunisia and Egypt enabled precisely the mobile interface effect that Farman describes, but in a way that enabled the political subjectivation process in a disembodied manner. A protester sending real time updates to Twitter enabled a connection with the wider online audience which could reveal that protester as a unique individual with a unique story, rather than as just another member of a faceless mass of protesting bodies. Mobile computing is interesting politically in that it can enable one to remain active in two spaces at once, rather than merely enhancing or augmenting one's experience in physical space. One can then be riding the train to work, a part of one's every day routine and thoroughly unpolitical, while at the same time be using one's phone to access an online political realm, allowing one to be a political subject even when one's body is busy with thoroughly non-political matters. By separating political participation from physical presence, politics can become more accessible, more pervasive, and easier to engage in. A politics of only bodies in seats or streets is one which introduces needless limitations on the ability to become a political subject.

The arguments relating to whether the internet is either embodied or disembodied tend to overwhelmingly commit the error of looking at one example from the software layer and then claiming that this example represents the essence of the hardware. Gies, for example, tries to argue that, with the proliferation of broadband internet and its capacity to enable forms of communication such as video and voice, the old text-based internet is left behind, meaning that the internet is now and will increasingly become embodied (Gies 2008, 321). The political consequences are then that the disembodied subjectivity argued for here becomes as difficult online as it is offline. Gies' argument is problematic because he is referring to the internet as a whole. Like the arguments of virtually every cybertheorist, from Turkle to Dean and from Stone to Gray, Gies fails to appreciate the complexity of cyberspace and the radically different forms of interaction which are determined not by the hardware, but by the type of website. On a website such as Chatroulette, which is a video chat service which connects users at random, the relation with others is pure embodiment in that most users either decide to hit next to talk to someone else or initiate a conversation based on the first few seconds of viewing the other user's video and therefore body. By contrast, a text-based discussion site such as Reddit with its large forums with millions of users dedicated to world news, global politics, and the politics of various countries, the relationship between users is radically disembodied, as there are strict rules against revealing personal information. Clearly these two sites present radically different online experiences, as one is primarily text based and the other is primarily video based. To claim that the internet in general, meaning its hardware layer, inherently only produces one of these experiences is simply wrong as it denies the malleability of the software layer.

3.7 The Emergence of the Universal

After the subject strips away particular identities, the next step is emerging as a member of the universal people. An act becomes political at the point when it is able to finish the subject-formation process and elevate a specific claim into a universal stand-in for any and all wrongs. As Žižek puts it,

> the situation becomes politicized when this particular demand starts to function as a metaphoric condensation of the global opposition against Them, those in power, so that the protest is no longer actually just about that demand, but about the universal dimension that resonates in that particular demand (2008a, 243).

A protest or complaint must move from being about something particular, which only applies to a small segment of the population, into something that serves to represent all complaints and problems with the existing order, thus moving from the realm of the social to the political. Politics is

> the art of the local and singular construction of cases of universality. Such construction is only possible as long as the singularity of the wrong…is distinguished from the particularization of right attributed to collectivities according to their identity (Rancière 1999, 139).

What this means is that for a protest or complaint to be properly political, it must be addressed to the whole and be able to serve as a metaphor for all instances of injustice. If the protest or complaint remains focused on incorporating an identity group into the whole, then it remains within the realm of the social. If a protest requires a certain identity to take part, then it fails to be political as it remains within the realm of social particularity.

'The people' who populate the political world have no positive identifications or qualifications such as virtue or wealth, just the empty indicator of freedom (Rancière 1999, 8). As Rancière puts it:

> Whoever has no part—the poor of ancient times, the third estate, the modern proletariat—cannot in fact have any part other than all or nothing…it is through the existence of this part of those who have no part, of this nothing that is all, that the community exists as a *political* community—that is, as divided by a fundamental dispute, by a dispute to do with the counting of the community's parts even more than of their 'rights' [emphasis added] (Rancière 1999, 9).

The fact that becoming a political subject does not require one to have a certain set of beliefs, qualifications, or a specific identity means that subjectivity strips away such things and one becomes part of those with no part. The part with no part has no identity and thus is not assigned a place in the hierarchically constructed order, yet it remains in existence floating alongside the established order. The lack of identity or qualifications means that it can claim to be the whole community–'the people'–precisely because it does not require any positive qualification. The political subject as the part with no part differs in this sense from both the Enlightenment subject, which had a single set of positive qualifications and identity traits which were falsely claimed to be universal, and the postmodern subject which is based on a multitude of different sets of positive identity qualifications.

An example of the subject-formation process which operated according to the logic of taking a particular and universalizing it into a metaphor for all complaints against the regime occurred during the Arab Spring. In Tunisia the initial catalyst for the protests and revolution came from a fruit vendor who, after facing police harassment and silence from authorities after he tried to complain, set himself on fire in a dramatic act of desperate suicide. This fruit vendor, Mohamed Bouazizi, had a specific complaint against a particular wrong, but the protests which later arose were not focused on the specific situation of fruit vendors and their mistreatment by police and the authorities. Instead Bouazizi became a metaphorical stand-in on to which everyone was able to project their various problems and complaints with the Tunisian regime. His treatment was elevated to a universal with which everyone could identify with, to the point where (untrue) rumours were even spread that he possessed a university degree in computer science but due to the government's corruption and lack of economic prospects was forced to sell fruit instead. In this way he became an emblem for the lower class, the middle class, and even those wealthier Tunisians who identified with him as a business owner frustrated by corruption and harassment from the authorities. The same type of metaphorical elevation happened in Egypt where one of the primary websites used by activists was called 'We Are all Khaled Said', invoking the idea that the mistreatment of one was the mistreatment of all. The success of the Arab Spring relied precisely on this inherently political move of elevating a particular wrong into an empty universal canvas onto which the people could project whatever complaints they had. One could imagine that, if the protests remained firmly about the particular situation of Tunisia's fruit vendors, the government could have easily either dismissed the protests as irrelevant to the wider Tunisian population or made some token move to marginally alleviate their situation and assert the rights of fruit vendors and thus appease the protesters, preventing the mass demonstrations that followed.

Given the recent history of North Africa and the Middle East, in which Islamism seemed to be the only organized form of popular resistance to the left-over dictatorships of the days of anti-colonial Arab nationalism, the stripping of specific identity to form a people is all the more striking. Perhaps the most widely used slogan during the Arab Spring was 'Ash-sha'b yurīd isqāṭ an-niẓām' which translates to 'the people wants to bring down the regime' (Abulof 2011). As Uriel Abulof points out, the inclusion of the term 'the people' is of utmost importance because

> in the two long centuries since Napoleon landed in Alexandria, the moral foundation of modern politics–popular sovereignty–has been absent from the Arab Middle East. The Arab people became the object for colonizers, dictators and imams, with their call to submission and arms. Never a subject for thought and action, the people lacked political agency, powerless to forge a collective moral self, let alone a nation to demand self-determination: the right to tell right from wrong in the public sphere (Abulof 2011).

By making the slogan specifically state that 'the people' want to bring down the regime, and not simply 'down with the regime,' is to declare the existence of a form of universal subjectivity. Furthermore, such a subjectivity had gone through the process of withdrawal and stripped itself of particular aspects. Many reports cite the ease with which Coptics and Muslims put aside religious differences to work together against the regime and how middle class professionals fought street battles hand in hand with the poor, as their various reasons for protesting the Egyptian dictatorship united them regardless of their private backgrounds (Alexander 2011, 8).

This form of universal subjectivity differs from the way the Syrian Islamists view themselves in the civil war that sprang out of the Arab Spring protests in that country. They transformed the slogan of 'the people wants to bring down the regime' to 'al-Ummah turīd khilāfah islāmiyyah' which translates to 'the Ummah wants an Islamic caliphate' (Sawah 2013). For the Syrian Islamists, it is not an empty universal people who want something but the ummah, which has a connotation of a specifically identified group: a nation of Muslims (Phillips 2012). Furthermore, they do not simply want the fall of the regime of President Bashir al-Assad but they specifically want an Islamic Caliphate, which is a form of government for and by a particular identity in which others would be excluded. While the Syrian uprising has its roots in the Arab Spring, the transformation of the slogan demonstrates that the war in Syria is now of a fundamentally different character than of the Arab Spring. The subjective emergence of an empty universal known simply as 'the people,' which was part of the reason the Arab Spring was such a unique event in the first place has been lost to the championing of particular identities. By universalizing a particular, the universal comes into effect not through subjects obtaining some supposedly neutral position but through recognizing and elevating to universality a particular that is out of joint or structurally excluded from the whole (Žižek 2008a, 269–270).

The uniting factor of this universality comes from the fact that each subject recognizes the inadequacy of any particular identity and thus throws his or her lot in with 'the people' who do not have a set of specific values to which one must adhere in order to become one of them (Žižek 2008b, 673). To be a part of the people who wants to bring down the regime meant being united with the other people as part of a collective, yet at the same time the people make no identity demands of the subjects, unlike the Syrian Islamists who demand a particular identity as a condition of participation. While subjects withdraw from identity, they do not lose their subjective and pluralistic opinions. In fact, it is precisely the stripping away of identity that allows each subject to be both universal and unique. For the Syrian Islamists, to identify as a Muslim and be part of their group means to also adhere to a set of dogmatic principles and values which are not open to debate, thus erasing plurality (van Tets 2014). Thus to maintain identity is to allow oneself to become just like everyone else, while the stripping away of identity allows the subject to reveal him or herself as a unique individual, allowing plurality to flourish. Consequently, when Judith Butler critiques the universal as a site of violent erasure, Žižek points out that this is not a critique of the universal but precisely its benefit (Žižek 2008a, 272). The universal as a site of erasure enables one to move beyond the static group constraints of cultural, bodily, or religious identification.

The universal as a site of violently erasing identity was the primary political move in ancient Athens which allowed for the development of democracy in the first place. In the reforms of Cleisthenes, *ethnos* was replaced by *demos*, where the *ethnos* is particular identity and the *demos* is universal political subjectivity. Unfortunately, however, *ethnos* is becoming more prominent today as wars break out over religious difference and multicultural society is predicated on assigning each identity a particular place so that there is no universal part with no part, but only a collection of well-ordered ethnic parts which come together to form a consensual whole with no polemical remainder. Even worse is the assumption that such ethnic identities are natural and inescapable, when in reality they are arbitrary to the point of bizarre. Many of the supposedly inheritable ethnic identities today which people claim are passed from parent to child are not even grounded in bodily traits or genetics, but in beliefs such as religion or nationality, so that the only way to discover someone's allegedly natural identity is to have them tell you. Rancière links this strange elevation of beliefs to the level of ethnic identity to the seemingly random categorization of animals in an ancient Chinese encyclopedia which is cited in a story by Jorge Luis Borges (Rancière 2010a, 4). Does the division of people into ethnicities such as Muslim, female, atheist, or immigrant not appear just as odd as dividing animals into categories such as those who belong to the Emperor, those who have just broken a pitcher, or those who act like madmen?

Too often these forms of naturalized identity are then used to disqualify the possibility for political subjectivation. As Prozorov argues,

> such familiar claims that e.g. equality is an impossibility in Islamic society or that Russian culture is hostile to freedom would be utterly irrelevant even if they were true, since world politics is not determined by any particular culture or tradition but is rather made possible by a subtraction from it (Prozorov 2014, 38).

Such naturalization of cultural identity is inherently anti-political as it attempts to erase the ability to act. As we have seen in everything from the revolts in Tunisia and Egypt to the activism of the band Pussy Riot in Russia, political action and the generation of political subjects is always possible everywhere, as the ability to say no is universal and requires no positive identifications. Thus when cultural relativists claim that one cannot criticize oppression or inequality in other cultures because of different practices, they are taking a strong stance against the possibility for political subjects to emerge within those cultures who can make a declaration that there is a wrong that must be negated, resulting in an anti-political attitude that ends up siding with the authorities and against political activists.

What the institutions of anti-politics attempt to do through a process of identifying such seemingly strange and arbitrary naturalized groups is to prevent 'the possibility of a 'metaphoric' elevation of particular wrong into a stand-in for the universal 'wrong" (Žižek 2008a, 243). This is done by deploying experts, social workers, and a discourse of tolerance to catalogue and identify the specifics of the situation in order to provide some recourse. The possibility of subjectivation and politicization are then precluded, yet the solutions provided are never quite satisfying and the possibility of destructive violence when the political is foreclosed always remains latent (Žižek 2008a, 242). In this sense, the assertion of a multiplicity of identities and a focus on cultural difference reinforces the dominant anti-political ideology of globalized capitalism, which happily adapts to the particularities of each culture, as this is more profitable than attempting to Americanize the world. Empty universality is thus the true opposite to the particular globalization of neoliberal capitalism.

3.8 Anonymity and the Harsh Light of the Public Sphere

If the political subject strips away identity with the help of disembodied online anonymity, how can a seemingly anonymous subject emerge to be universally recognized and speak to the entire public? There would seem to be a contradiction between the idea of hiding our private identities online through anonymity while at the same time revealing ourselves as politically unique individuals. The most common method of recognizing people in the offline world is through their bodies. Thus if subjectivity reveals us as unique individuals, the argument goes that we need a face to attach to the stories revealed by political speech and action in order for it to be remembered and have impact. The idea of a body as identifier is problematic for a number of reasons, especially if we consider identical twins who cannot be bodily distinguished. If one twin accomplishes some great feat, we do not simply ignore it or forget it because there is another person who looks exactly like him or her. As Arendt argues, what is really needed to accompany political subjectivity is a name rather than a body, as speech is attached to a 'who' rather than a 'what' (Arendt 1998, 181). But even if it is accepted that a body is not needed to be revealed in the subjectivation process, the question of internet anonymity remains: how can one reveal oneself while at the same time being anonymous?

For outspoken critics of the internet, such as Hubert Dreyfus, the supposed anonymity and disembodied nature of not just online political discussion, but the internet in general, is posited as an insurmountable obstacle to the revealing of an online political subjectivity (Dreyfus 2008). While Dreyfus is another in a long list of thinkers who confuse the hardware and software layers, leading to proclamations about the internet as a whole, as if all websites were exactly alike, his bigger problem is attempting to link anonymity to a lack of commitment. He argues that online anonymous interactions simply lack the passion necessary for politics due to anonymity and even claims that on the internet 'nothing matters enough that one would be willing to die for it' (Dreyfus 2008, 73). Against the background of the internet-integrated revolutions in Tunisia and Egypt which resulted in many deaths of protesters who were passionately engaged in a political cause they were willing to die for, this claim holds little weight, especially when linked to the question of anonymity. As I argue in the chapter on conflict, the ability to protect one's private identity online by engaging politically through a pseudonym can enhance conflictual political engagement as the lack of repercussions in one's private life leads to people being more willing to express dissent and unpopular opinions. Furthermore, groups such as Anonymous engage in hacking operations online at great risk to their own freedom, as cybercrime continues to be disproportionately punished (Murfin 2014; Fakhoury 2014). Dreyfus also argues that the internet's anonymity empowers 'anonymous experts' to provide their opinions on anything from a position of 'nowhere' thus creating a levelling effect which erases all relevance and significance (Dreyfus 2008, 78–79). Such hyperbole simply uses the novelty of the technology as a means to launch into an attack on politics itself. The real problem with online anonymity for Dreyfus is actually that of the political subject as an empty universal whose only qualification to participate politically is that they have no qualification.

Returning to the bigger question of how one might reveal oneself as a unique subject in the context of online anonymity, requires returning to the process of subjectivity and how it operates. The first step is the stripping of identity, which makes the subject anonymous. However, the process does not end here, as many critics would seem to imply. Stripping away particularities allows the subject to emerge on a universal level and speak as an individual rather than as an object. In this sense, very little online speech and interaction is truly anonymous, as people's speech is associated with a consistent name. Even the hacktivist movement Anonymous is not truly anonymous, as it operates under a collective pseudonym which maintains a name allowing a political story surrounding their actions to emerge. If the movement was truly anonymous, no one other than those directly involved would have any idea who was performing the various online actions and any kind of political impact would be lost, as there would be no public story to be told. When people go online and strip away their identities, they are only briefly anonymous, as once they start to engage with others they begin to reveal a subjective political narrative that is attached to a pseudonym. When one signs up with a discussion site or chat room, one creates a new name to associate their speech with, a name that comes to be associated with various opinions and actions.

The construction of online subjectivity through the use of pseudonyms helps maintain a public voice which, at the same time, protects private identity. Pseudonymous speech and action has a long history, and is not simply an issue of online interaction. In the nineteenth century, female authors often used pseudonyms in order to ensure their works would be evaluated based on their merit and not on the gender of the authors.[6] In periods of upheaval activists would often adopt pseudonyms to protect their own private identities. Prior to the October Revolution in Russia in 1917, Vladimir Ilyich Ulyanov and Lev Davidovich Bronstein adopted the pseudonyms of Lenin and Trotsky to initially protect their private identities. Pseudonyms were pervasive during the French resistance to Nazi occupation (Colonel Rèmy, Vercors), as well as during the American Revolution and its aftermath, with examples of the pseudonym Publius used for the publication of *The Federalist Papers* and Thomas Paine, who published a number of pamphlets under the pseudonym 'Common Sense'.

To protect themselves from state persecution for blasphemy, atheist critics of Islam have adopted pseudonyms when publishing books and writing online.[7] When dissent threatens the security of one's body, then the ability to speak politically requires mechanisms to hide bodily identity. Pseudonymity helps ensure that a wide range of views can be expressed publicly by protecting those with outsider opinions from the tyranny of the majority and from state repression. The ability to obscure one's offline and private identity when speaking politically online makes politics safer and more inclusive, as it takes a great deal of courage to enter the public sphere and reveal oneself to the world. Arendt argues that courage is the primary political virtue precisely because it is not easy to reveal oneself if what is being revealed is disagreeable to what the majority thinks (Arendt 1998, 36). Online politics can reduce the risk to the body, and make political participation more accessible by disconnecting one's public persona from one's private life. Doing so enables people to speak politically with less fear of negative ramifications for one's employment, safety, or social relations. For this reason, Facebook and other social networking sites which tend to insist on real names are poorly suited to become the seeds of an online political realm, while more pseudonymous sites like Reddit, which lack the identifying aspects of having a profile with pictures and personal information, do present such a nascent model of online political subjectivity.

Political and pseudonymous cyberspaces challenge the entire concept of a unitary and true identity in their ability to split the public persona of political subjectivity from the private persona (Saco 2002, 130). This ability to be two people at once disrupts the anti-political method of identification, surveillance, counting, and putting in place. Whether the anti-political state operates based on Plato's *sophrosyne*, in which people must mind their own business and stay in their assigned place, or through panoptic surveillance, as described by Foucault, which operates by making bodies visible, the ability to create a second life which is split away from the body and its associated classifications enables political speech and undermines anti-political devices. When it is argued that online pseudonymity simply provides a cover for immoral and illegal behaviour (not dissimilar to Plato's story about the ring of Gyges), the point of pseudonymity and its political implications is missed (Saco 2002, 117). Someone's political speech, whether online or offline, reveals who one is more than one's bodily identity, and thus when people act crude and boorish online they are revealing who they truly are, not becoming someone else because they think they can get away with anything in online space. At the same time, so long as they act under pseudonyms, their poor behaviour will follow them online and reveal them to everyone as a crude and boorish individual. While online anonymity can certainly enable crime (Choo and Smith 2008), this is not an argument against online space per se, as all crime must be anonymous regardless of what kind of space it takes place within. No one robs a bank wearing a shirt that displays one's name and address.

The story that reveals us as unique subjects is not consciously created by us, even though it arises out of our political speech and action. It is always hidden to us as it is dependent on how other people interpret and perceive it. The stories that are generated through our online political interactions are not the creation of an identity from scratch, as, try as we might to come across in a certain way, the political subject that we reveal has an unconscious character.

Thus, online political subjectivity is not about crafting a new identity but about revealing our innermost thoughts to others which constitute us as unique individuals. While this can often be difficult due to the sheer volume of comments and the often anti-political mechanisms of public relevance algorithms, the opportunities to reveal our political subjectivity online are greatly enhanced over offline space. The increased ability to express our own views within the context of a larger movement, such as within Occupy, is a positive improvement over the totalizing movements of the past. Whether in the form of communist parties requiring a certain ideological adherence or the identity social movements which erased subjectivity in favour of identity, individuals were subsumed into a mass movement leaving little room for individuals to reveal their own uniqueness. With the help of the internet, we can now both be part of larger movements and assert our own subjectivity, thus affirming the plurality of politics.

3.9 Anti-Political Identification versus Political Subjectivation

Seeing as subjectivity is a terrain of contestation between politics and anti-politics, a more precise elaboration of how identity is used by anti-politics to foreclose subjectivity is needed, and on this I will draw on Rancière and place him in contrast to Althusser and Foucault. Part of the recent impetus for rejecting notions of political subjectivity comes from the influential accounts of Althusser and Foucault who treat the political subject not as a free actor but as someone who is subjected to the state. For Althusser, the subject is interpellated by ideology, and thus 'the individual is interpellated as a (free) subject in order that he shall submit freely to the commandments of the Subject, i.e. in order that he shall (freely) accept his subjection' (Althusser 2008, 56). Foucault and the theorists of governmentality, such as Nikolas Rose, extend the Althusserian idea so that subjects are produced by the application of biopower through the management of populations in prisons, clinics, schools, and virtually all aspect of life (Rose 1999). Again, subjects are subjected and produced by the government in order to assent to its structure. This is not subjectivity but identity, and it relates not to politics but to what Rancière calls 'policing'. A proper form of subjectivity is not a positive placing in a specific world, as in Althusser and Foucault, but a subtraction from it which enables access to the empty universal world. The problem with Althusserian or Foucauldian accounts of subjectivity as identification relates to how anyone can break out of this subjection and act politically, a question that Foucault did turn to in later in life, but a question which Rancière is much better equipped to deal with.

In Rancière's terminology, politics is bound up with the police, where politics introduces dissensus and disagreement and the role of the police is maintaining the existing consensual distribution of the sensible. Policing the status quo consists of keeping all the multiple identities that make up the social whole in their assigned places. The primary move of the anti-political police is to deny the existence of the part with no part (Rancière 1999, 14). The idea that the whole of the community might be more than the sum of its parts, that individuals may transcend the boundaries of their given social, economic, or political position is intolerable, as it opens up access to the universal realm of politics to anyone. The key innovation of democracy is that politics is not simply a job, or a specific role in society only open to those who are qualified, but that politics is universally relevant, as its debates and decisions affect everyone. Politics requires no specific qualification or identity to take part, and thus the part with no part are those who have no qualification, assigned place, or specific identity. The part with no part stake this lack of qualification to be precisely what gives them the right to take part in public politics. It is precisely this subjectivation process which removes assigned places and allows access to the universal that anti-politics seeks to foreclose by asserting and policing identity and status.

While politics has been traditionally thought of as the set of procedures whereby the aggregation and consent of collectivities is achieved, power is organized, places and roles are distributed, and various systems are designed to legitimize these distributions are devised, these functions are properly anti-political (Rancière 1999, 28). Anti-politics distributes bodies into places, and then designs systems to ensure that those bodies stay where they are put. A body is placed based on its properties which constitute an identity, rather than on the subjectivity of the unique person who inhabits the body (Rancière 1999, 27). Thus 'to put someone in his/her place' is a prime expression of anti-politics, as it involves discovering someone's identity and using it to dismiss a person's claim to speak to the universal of politics. Political activity threatens the anti-political counting of parts and distributing of places by allowing individuals to move out of their assigned place and access the political realm. So long as one has access to a political space which is universal in its lack of required identity or qualifications to take part, one can become a political subject and be more than whatever occupation, identity, or social position such a person is assigned to by the police. The universality of politics and the shifting places of political subjects is viewed as a threat to both the stability of the anti-political order and the elite-based mode of government that radically alienates the vast majority from taking part in politics.

Like Žižek, Rancière makes an explicit link between political subjectivity and Cartesian subjectivity. The Cartesian subject's being is derived from its capacity to think, not from the identity of its body, social position, or economic value. In this sense 'any subjectification is a disidentification, removal from the naturalness of a place, the opening up of a subject space where anyone can be counted since it is the space where those of no account are counted' (Rancière 1999, 36). Rancière provides the example of the revolutionary Auguste Blanqui who was put on trial in 1832. The judge asked his profession and he simply replied 'proletarian', to which the judge responded by claiming that is not a profession, which allowed Blanqui to make the political claim that it is the profession of millions of people who live off their labour but are denied political rights (Rancière 1999, 37). The judge is following the anti-political logic of identification, trying to identify Blanqui and thus put him in his place as someone unqualified to take a political stand. Blanqui on the other hand refuses to fall for the attempt at identification and instead simply posits himself as a member of an identity-less collectivity that lacks any specific properties but is open to anyone who claims their rights are being infringed upon by the current state of French government. The vexation experienced by the judge at the declaration of proletarian as profession relates to the fact that within politics subjects do not have consistent bodies. They are, as Rancière calls them, 'fluctuating performers' (Rancière 1999, 89).

Anti-political society can be thought of as an aggregation and collection of identities, in which there is no real 'majority', just a lot of minorities who, once collated, form a whole. The subjectivation process, which involves a stripping away of these assigned identities, is an emancipation from the state of being a minority (Rancière 2011, 42). It is on this account that defence of identity as political yet again fails to be politically transformative and ends up having the anti-political effect of keeping people in their places and cutting them off from political action. The goal of political feminism for example must be to declassify and de-identify gender as a political (dis)qualification. Those who attempt to assert the primacy of gender, even when meaning well, by arguing in favour of electoral schemes which, for example, might provide a quota that guarantees women will have half the seats in parliament, simply reduce a woman to her gender identity. Any political argument about gender equality is then reduced to a matter of the distribution and policing of the parts, thus foreclosing the emancipation from gender identity and the move from member of identity group to political subject capable of revealing herself as a unique individual who is not defined by her body or identity.

The subjectivation process of declassification, disidentification, and emergence from a state of minority also speaks to the method of politics in its oppositional form. In so far as the subject-formation process is political, it operates in a manner that seeks to affirm universal equality rather than uncover more and more inequalities. Continuing to use feminism as an example, the case of Jeanne Deroin is exemplary in demonstrating how the political subjectivation process seeks to affirm universal equality and thus declassify identity as a qualification or class that hinders political involvement. In 1849 Deroin presented herself as a candidate for the national election in France, even though at the time it was illegal for a woman to take a seat in French parliament (Rancière 1999, 41). She ran on the presumption that the universal equality guaranteed to all in the French Constitution was not merely a lie meant to cover over the fact that equality was only for a specific gender identity. Her action began with the assumption of equality and set about to put that formal statement of equality to the test, knowing full well she was demonstrating a contradiction between what the constitution said, and what was reality (Rancière 1999, 41). In this sense, she sought to emancipate herself from the minority position of 'woman' by revealing herself as a unique individual with her own opinions that made her worthy of taking part in the universal discourse of politics through her act of running for office. Subjectivity is not merely a demand on the other, but a proof to oneself that one is not limited by social, economic, cultural, or bodily identity and that one is a unique individual capable of engaging with others as a political subject (Rancière 2007, 48). In this sense Deroin proved to herself, and everyone else, that through her campaign she was the equal of the men running, and that therefore the wrong existed not in the declaration of universal equality, but in the fact that this equality was not being put into practice.

This political method of affirming and asserting equality is in direct contrast to the method of arguing that the contradiction between the formal equality of the constitution and what is experienced proves that the claim to formal universal equality a lie. The latter method, which has unfortunately been adopted by much of the Left as part of the general sentiment against universal subjectivity, plays into the hands of the anti-political order by affirming inequality. If statements of universal equality are simply ideological lies, and the job of the Left is to expose those lies, then there is no political action to be undertaken but simply a demand that the forces of anti-politics be more efficient at parcelling up society based on identity. What uncovering more and more inequalities as a political method amounts to, is a demand for more surveillance, control, and policing (Dean 2009, 7). The part with no part, which is the basis of political subjectivity, is denied as a possibility and the job of the activist becomes uncovering new forms of inequality rather than generating more equality. It is on this register that the suspicion of universality in favour of particular identity that has become fashionable on the Left makes it an unwitting ally of the anti-politics of everything from Christian fundamentalists to marketing campaigns which rely on selling niche products to specific identity groups (Dean 2009, 8–9).

In so far as the subject moves beyond identity, I do not wish to simply dismiss identity issues as politically irrelevant. At the same time, the empty subject does not lose private identity altogether, but merely keeps it private so as to be able to speak universally without such private attachments becoming grounds for disqualification. As was noted earlier, the emergence of the universal quite often stems from taking a particular injustice as a metaphorical stand-in for all injustices. Identity issues can be elevated to be metaphorical stand-ins, so long as those of the specific identity in question are willing to allow their particular issue to move beyond their own particular concerns. The early days of the gay rights movement provides a good example as one of the most prominent slogans was 'gay rights are human rights', which explicitly attempted to use the wrongs against gays and lesbians as a stand-in for any person who was being denied basic human rights. In this sense, many identity issues are properly political in so far as they aim for depoliticizing identity. While a political movement for depoliticization may sound contradictory, there is also the paradoxical sounding anti-political move toward politicization. Same-sex marriage and abortion are two examples of issues which should not be political matters, as they are matters of basic individual rights and not of public concern. The movement to depoliticize and, thus, keep these issues a matter of private choice is thoroughly political in so far as it involves attempting to politically declassify women and gays as identity groups to be publicly acted on. By contrast, when conservative groups try to make these issues a matter of public concern, they often portray their moves as simply a matter of invoking a political debate, but making identity into a matter of public concern is, as I have argued throughout this chapter, a fundamental move of anti-politics meant to deny political subjectivity so that people can be treated as homogenous groups to be parcelled and policed, and thus treated as objects. If politics is thought of as a stage, then in addition to the speech and action of those on it, politics also involves the boundary work of debating who gets to be on the stage in the first place, as well as deciding what should and should not be performed on the stage.

Online political subjectivity as an empty universal must also be considered in terms of the terrain of contestation between political subjectivity and anti-political identity. As with all the four terrains which make up the understanding of politics advanced here, the terrain is configured as a sliding scale where less qualifications to become a subject make it more political. When considering such subjects in an online context, empirical qualifications related to access and ability to use the internet remain a problem. While the digital divide is becoming less about relative wealth and more about quality of internet access due to issues surrounding state censorship and net neutrality, disqualifications still exist that can prevent those who wish to engage online with others from doing so (Castells 2011). At the same time, the universality of online subjectivity faces barriers in terms of language. In the context of an online forum, the very lack of ability to prejudge someone because identity is hidden, can turn into a disqualification itself. Someone who joins such a forum for the first time may face obstacles for being unknown and having no commenting history. Although the internet can help overcome empirical obstacles to subjectivization related to prejudice, it also introduces new obstacles and points of qualification which must become sites of political dispute themselves. The goal of each terrain is to make it more political, while realizing that perfection or purity is likely an impossibility.

While some people may enter the online political realm and seek to fight off their own subjectivity and reproduce their identity online, at least in an online context their identity does not precede them. Someone who is part of an identity group who finds that group oppressive and totalizing has the option of hiding that identity online, something which is not as easy offline. Political emancipation means emerging from a minority and becoming part of the part with no part, whose only qualification is that it has no qualifications whatsoever. Thus when the advocates of online bodily identification argue that online activity quickly reproduces offline identity, as one is often asked about private characteristics in the course of an online political debate (Gies 2008), they miss the point that these are anti-political mechanisms which are meant to disqualify and oppress. Gies tries to argue that these common tactics demonstrate that we find talking to disidentified and disembodied actors as uncomfortable, but this is an attempt to naturalize a depoliticized discourse that only makes sense outside of political discussions. One only cares who one is talking to in a social context, a political statement is, by its nature, public and thus addressed toward everyone. It matters little toward whom political speech is directed, given that it is meant to be public. The lack of identity or body of those we engage with in a political context simply does not matter unless we want to look for ways to attempt to place, categorize, and identify our interlocutors as unqualified to take part in political discussion and thus deny their own subjectivity and right to participate.

Political subjectivity is about making the mind visible through the process of revealing subjectivity, a task that requires speech (whether that speech is oral, written, or electronically transmitted through fibre optic cables) and the construction of stories in order for it to be revealed. The focus on embodiment, as was pointed to in the last chapter, is overtly anti-political, as the body does not tell a story. It simply exists in its thereness, and to make political judgements based on the body is to deny individuals their uniqueness. Saco makes a useful contrast between political and anti-political forms of visibility by comparing Arendt and Foucault. For Arendt, what must become visible is the content of the person's mind, and this is liberating and intensely political, while for Foucault what becomes visible is the body as it becomes the object of surveillance and governmentality (Saco 2002, 132). In this sense, Foucault provides a depiction of the anti-political process of identification in which individuals are treated as bodies to be classified, counted, categorized, and treated as objects that are part of a population to be acted on. Online subjectivity is politically beneficial precisely because it can allow us to escape the anti-political regime of the management and surveillance of bodies in walled territories.

At the same time, however, the internet's openness, in the form of the malleability of the software layer, means that it can be adopted for anti-political purposes to reaffirm identity against subjectivity. Dean argues that the internet is characterized by the sovereign reign of 'subjectless flows of communication' which become the infrastructure for a new model of capitalism based on information exchange (Dean 2003, 104). On this register, she speaks about how certain websites are becoming more and more tailored to individual users, to the point where a news site might not show any news that a user might find upsetting or disagreeable, thus undermining universality and actually isolating people in their particularities (Dean 2009, 45). What these examples point to is not an argument against the internet as a realm of subjectivity but its open and contested nature. In the same way that in-person public communication can be part of a political subject-formation process or can be part of an identification and particularizing process, the internet's software layer cannot be reduced to its hardware. No doubt more identification and particularizing methods will be developed for online use in order to make the internet seem less and less of a place where a public realm can be created which is fit for the formation of political subjects, but these are precisely the types of things which should be, and are, the topic of political debates and actions which legitimately can lead to political subjectivity arising online. The fact the internet might be used for anti-political purposes now is no reason to dismiss it so long as it still has the potential to be used for political purposes.

The political subject formation process involves stripping away identity in order to enable the formation of an empty universal in which political participation requires no status qualifications. What political subjects have in common is literally nothing, which keeps the subject formation process open and available to all. While identity concerns plague offline politics, such private concerns can more easily be set aside online where such identities are less obvious when subjects adopt pseudonyms and make an effort to keep these identities concealed. Online subjectivity and its seemingly initial anonymity are conducive to political subjectivity, as it lets one easily begin the process of revealing oneself to others as a unique individual. The initial anonymity, quickly replaced by pseudonymity, obscures the body and prevents the various bodily prejudices such as racism or sexism from disqualifying one's speech before one ever has a chance to speak. This, in turn, allows one's speech to start from a clean slate, allowing the subject's opinions to speak for themselves, while at the same time protecting the publicly revealed political subject's body and private identity from attacks and discrimination based on these revealed political opinions. As I will argue in the next two chapters, this political subject operating within an online political realm can vastly improve political participation and the pluralistic conflict of opinions that form the content of political debate. The manner in which online subjectivity facilitates political subjectivity means that not only can it not be claimed that politics online is inferior or less real, but that an online politics may provide a number of key advantages over offline politics. With the case of political subjectivity, accomplishing it online makes the process easier and safer, which can help enable reinvigorating the practice of the political.

CHAPTER 4

Participation

4.1 Critiquing Representation

In the previous chapters the concept of the political realm was established, which then led to theorizing the nature of the political subjects who enter it. The next two chapters will deal with the critical question of what these political subjects in an online political realm actually do. This chapter will address the broader concept of political participation and what it entails, both at the theoretical level and how it would operate online, while the next chapter will deal with the conflict generated by such participation. While, on the surface, participation may seem like a relatively uncontroversial issue, as it is the basis of the concept of democracy, deeper questions lurk below this surface which are related to who gets to participate and in what capacity. The dominant system of representative democracy seeks to constrain public participation to peripheral matters related to selecting who gets sent to the legislature, which leaves the public outside of the political realm by denying their participation in political debates and decisions. While theories of more engaged forms of democratic participation have circulated as a theoretical alternative, there has long been a dominant feeling that such schemes are unworkable except in small communities with a very limited number of possible participants (Rousseau 2003, 45; Montesquieu 1989, 124). Given that the internet has the capacity to break down constraints on time and space that are usually cited as the primary obstacles to more participatory forms of democracy, this chapter argues that the internet demands a theoretical rethink of what forms of political participation may now be practically possible.

The protest movements of Occupy and the Arab Spring, like most protest movements before them, demonstrate the continued significance of participation as a terrain of conflict between politics and anti-politics, as these movements operated on a model of mass participation in which anyone could simply

---

How to cite this book chapter:

Smith, T. G. 2017. *Politicizing Digital Space: Theory, The Internet, and Renewing Democracy.* Pp. 71–97. London: University of Westminster Press. DOI: https://doi. org/10.16997/book5.d. License: CC-BY-NC-ND 4.0

join the protests and act in a political manner. While the idea of mass participation in politics is not unique to protest movements, as elections rely on the same principle, the protest movements do operate on a model of participation that is more meaningful than simply casting a ballot. Even though protests can often be as infrequent as elections, they demonstrate a latent possibility and desire for a more meaningful form of participation. It is this desire to participate in the affairs of politics, to be able to enter the political realm and to reveal oneself as a unique individual, which has driven much protest in the past. Yet, it is a desire that never seems to be sustained. The Arab Spring successfully topples dictators but dissipates into military and Islamist-led governments. Occupy fades away, leaving its participants having made a crucial point but no more able to participate in public affairs. It is at this point that the significance of the internet for political participation cannot be underestimated. If the political realm need not be a physical space, then the dispersion of a protest does not have to mean the end of the opportunity to participate in an alternative political space, and an election need not be the only time citizens are given the chance to have input into how the government operates.

Before getting into the issue of online politics, a critique of representative democracy is required, in part because this system has come to be seen as the only legitimate form of democracy. Unlike the word politics, the word democracy has an overall positive connotation to it. As Hay points out, politics has come to have the meaning of government by deception and conjures up negative feelings, while democracy is becoming more accepted as the best form of government (Hay 2007, 8–32). Any meaningful definition of democracy that is to include all of its diverse and often radically divergent forms must centre on the idea that it involves some form of citizen participation, whether in the form of voting in elections, discussing issues in a public sphere, or direct participation in decision making. In this manner, the idea of participation itself is not opposed by anti-politics, as democracy is increasingly viewed as the only legitimate form of government. The shape which participation takes, however, does stake out participation as a major terrain of contestation between politics and anti-politics. Representative democracy, which has become the global standard for legitimate government, is predicated on reducing mass participation to a very minimum level, so that participation is pushed to the periphery either in the form of voting or other activities related to elections, or in the occasional outburst of a protest. The opportunities to participate remain few and far between.

The problems with representative government are not new, but its hegemonic ideological position as the only legitimate form of government in popular discourse have made these problems fade into the background, as alternatives are deemed either impractical or undesirable. Even Thomas Jefferson, writing in the early days of representative democracy, feared that it might turn into 'elective despotism,' as the American Constitution excluded the American people from entering the political realm (cited in Arendt 2006b, 230). Jefferson feared this exclusion of all but the representatives would lead the American people to lose interest in public affairs, transforming the representatives into rulers, and making politicians into wolves who act not at the behest of those who elected them but according to their own interests (Arendt 2006b, 230). In many ways, Jefferson's fears have come to pass, as 'Marx's once-scandalous thesis that governments are simple business agents for international capital is today obvious fact on which 'liberals' and 'socialists' agree' (Rancière 1999, 113). As Rancière goes on to argue, managing the economy is how governments claim legitimacy, when this used to be considered a secret to obscure (Rancière 1999, 113). Politicians not actually doing a proper job of representing the interests of those who elected them is, however, more of a problem with how representative democracy functions in a practical sense, but there are much deeper theoretical problems with it.

The claim that democracy empowers the people so that governments act not on the model of coercive force, such as in monarchy or despotism, but are organs of the people holds true, essentially, only on election day. The ability to participate in choosing those who will go on to have exclusive access to the space in which decisions are made is better than not having this choice but still alienates virtually all citizens from the political realm. In this manner, the ability to choose one's boss is better than not having that ability, but it is clearly inferior to being able to participate in the decision making process and, thus, not being subject to the decisions of others. Representative government diminishes political space and provides no realm where people can be seen in political action (Arendt 2006b, 229). This radical alienation from participating in the debates and decisions that affect everyone leads to a reassertion of the difference between those who are ruled and those who rule, which the anti-monarchic revolutions in France and the United States had sought to undo (Arendt 2006b, 229). The ability to participate in politics is pushed outside of the realm of decision and, at best, the people can debate and protest amongst themselves, but the decision making authority rests solely in the hands of the elected officials.

Since direct participation is considered practically impossible by advocates of representative democracy, the best a person can hope for is to be represented, but what does it mean to be represented? If individuals are unique subjects, with unique opinions, how can one person represent a plural group of political subjects, all of whom have different and possibly conflicting opinions? Groups cannot form opinions because this would require everyone in the group to think exactly alike, something which is impossible and undesirable. Furthermore, a group cannot argue or debate, as this is only possible among individuals. What gets represented instead, are the moods and interests of a group (Arendt 2006b, 260–261). As Arendt explains, voters then make their choice according to their private lives and personal interests and act to try to influence the elected official to act in accordance with one's own interests, while at the same time every other person is attempting to do the same. In this manner, Arendt likens voting to 'the reckless coercion with which a blackmailer forces his victim into obedience', which in no way resembles the democracy of political 'power that arises out of joint action and joint deliberation' (Arendt 2006b, 261). Representation becomes, at best, the aggregation of moods and interests, and, at worst, the means by which the few are able to legitimize their control of the public policy agenda.

Even as early as 1963, when Arendt wrote *On Revolution*, she speaks of 'Madison Avenue methods' being introduced into elections which transformed them into a relation between buyer and seller, thus subsuming the political process into capitalist consumerism (Arendt 2006b, 268). Elections have increasingly become less and less about policy differences and more about marketing an image or brand to voters. With the rise of the Third Way and the general neo-liberal consensus, political parties have increasingly made election campaigns about the personal suitability of candidates, rather than about giving voters a choice between opposed policy directions. Even voting, the one official act of participation that is lauded as bestowing democratic legitimacy, is then depoliticized as it becomes harder to use one's vote to express a political choice. Representative government acts as a hollowed out body without organs, in which everyone claims fidelity to the idea that the people should participate in government, but the actual avenues to do so are extremely limited and without real substance.[8] By pushing people outside of the political body by constraining political space, the organs of political participation can still be claimed to be functional, but are made unavailable to the vast majority.

Rancière calls the anti-political mechanisms of representative democracy parapolitics, in that it seeks not to outwardly eliminate participation and conflict but merely displace them into other non-political realms (Rancière 1999, 72). Parapolitical representative democracy 'consists in redirecting the feverish energy activated on the public stage toward other ends, in sending it on a search for material prosperity, private happiness, and social bonds' (Rancière 2009b, 8). Notions of the public good are rendered subservient to private wealth, and the people's representatives become primarily concerned with promoting private prosperity. Public citizens are then replaced with a collection of self-interested private individuals only interested in their own wealth accumulation, a situation in which politics is replaced with 'collective housekeeping' (Arendt 1998, 28). When the system is designed to valorize economic participation and positions political participation as an unproductive distraction from economic activity, it is hardly any wonder why official voter participation rates are dropping.

The literature that seeks to find reasons why voter turnout numbers are at all-time lows and why the average person seems disinterested in government fails to realize that these 'problems' are directly generated by the nature of representative government itself, and not simply a problem of personal attitudes. Hay calls this a demand side approach to the problem, as it assumes there must be something wrong with citizens, rather than the system itself (Hay 2007, 39). Putnam puts most of the blame for declining voter participation on a loss of a sense of civic duty which relates to what he calls an overall decline in social capital (Putnam 2001). Norris points to the general increase in education and sophistication of the average voter as leading to what she calls 'critical citizens' who are less likely to vote because of this critical disposition (Norris 2011). Franklin argues that voting is a habit, and that the general decline in voter participation rates began when the voting age was lowered to 18. He goes on to argue that this younger demographic were less socially engaged and thus less likely to vote anyway, which led to the habit of not voting (Franklin 2004). In each of these arguments about why people are less likely to engage, there is almost no consideration of structural and systemic factors, as all of the analysis is aimed at explaining individual behaviour patterns. Democracy is cast as the ideal which politics subverts, when in reality the current mode of representative democracy is undermining politics itself (Hay 2007, 153).

4.2 Beyond Representation: Political Participation and the Metaphor of the Stage

The fundamental problem with representative democracy is that it excludes the people from participating in both debate and decision on any given issue. There are examples, however, such as in Switzerland and some individual American states, in which the people can vote directly in a referendum and thus can participate directly in a decision. This form of direct or plebiscite democracy is posited as a common alternative to representation, but still has serious flaws (Bowler and Donovan 2000; Cronin 1999). The main problem is that these opportunities to make decisions are provided without proper provisions for debate. Thus a question is posed to people who are not given a proper opportunity to discuss and debate it with others which would force them to consider a variety of perspectives which leads to creating an informed opinion. The recent Brexit referendum provides an example, in which the day after the UK voted to leave the EU, Google searches inside the UK asking what Brexit meant and what would happen if the UK did leave the EU skyrocketed. People searching for basic information after the vote had already happened, including 'What is the EU referendum?', demonstrate that at the very least the general public was less than fully informed about what the referendum was about (Walton 2016). Voting on issues without a proper understanding of what the issue is can hardly be considered an expression of democratic choice.

In this sense, referendums often serve to support the authority of the government and undermine change, especially if the referendum is framed as a yes or no question where the options are simply status quo or some form of change. Uninformed people who are simply presented a question on which they are expected to make a decision will have an inherent bias against change when they do not understand what the change will mean (LeDuc 2011). Referenda on electoral reform in Canada often suffer from this problem, as those who take the time to understand the issue realize the need for change, but those who have not looked into the issue will default to supporting the status quo. At the same time, referenda can be captured by a small motivated group when the issue is not compelling enough to ensure high voter turnouts. There can also be problems related to issues of minority rights (Gamble 1997). The classic example is women's suffrage, which was delayed in Switzerland by referenda until it was finally passed in 1971. A more recent example would be the 2008 California Proposition 8 ballot initiative which re-banned same-sex marriage.

If direct democracy is problematic because it results in decisions without debate, then deliberative democracy, as outlined by numerous academics including Gutmann and Thompson (2009), Habermas (1985), and Benhabib (1992), seems like a more reasonable model of democracy as it focuses on debate and deliberation. While positions vary within the broad umbrella of deliberative democratic theory, the common focus is that there should be a robust public sphere where people can go to deliberate on public affairs and thus create a more informed public opinion. People will ideally not be making rash decisions which can be easily manipulated by elites or the government, as their participation comes in the form of discussing and deliberating. The major problem with deliberative democracy, especially in the version presented by Gutmann and Thompson, is that it tends to still leave decision making in the hands of elected representatives. These representatives are supposed to act based on the informed public opinion generated through the deliberative process, but this is a crucial gap which leaves open the very real possibility that the representatives will simply ignore public opinion, as decision making authority ultimately rests with the representatives and not the public deliberators. The public sphere remains something entirely outside of the official realm of state politics, and all the participation in deliberation becomes more informative than decisive. Habermas positions deliberative democracy as a middle ground between liberal democracy (defined as the collation of private interests) and what he calls 'republican democracy', which is exemplified by Arendt's political theory. Even for Habermas deliberative democracy is positioned as weaker than an Arendtian participatory democracy and, thus, explicitly limits the participatory role of the citizen to the point where they are excluded from decisions (Habermas 1994a, 7).

Participation in politics must include both the means to participate in the opinion forming mechanisms of debate and deliberation as well as participating in the decision making process. Action without talk and talk without action are both problematic. Thus deliberative democracy and direct democracy are both inadequate on their own, as a properly participatory politics needs mechanisms to facilitate all means of politics, including speech, action, listening, and protest. When speaking of political participation theatrical metaphors are often invoked, from Arendt's claim that politics is 'virtuosity of performance' to Rancière's references to *mise en scène* and the staging of politics (Arendt 2006a, 152; Rancière 1999, 55). In this sense, a complete picture of political participation involves the actors on the stage who undertake debate and decision, the audience who listens and judges what happens on stage, and all of the off-stage drama that surrounds conflicts over who gets to be on the stage and what their role is.

The most elementary aspect of political participation is the ability to speak one's mind in a meaningful way that is taken seriously and listened to by others. Anti-political prejudice treats the people as a troublesome animal, capable of expressing pain and pleasure but not of engaging in meaningful speech that can express opinions (Rancière 1999, 22). Political science becomes the art of taming the beast of public sentiment, an art that remains relevant even when people are able to elect representatives and are guaranteed the right to freedom of speech. Thus before one can even express an opinion on a political issue, speech becomes a terrain of contestation between politics and anti-politics at the level of who is considered capable of speech, and who is simply making the noises of pleasure or pain. Before an actor can speak to the audience, a stage must be constructed which provides the opportunity for speech. Anti-politics denies such stages are necessary because the masses do not speak, they only signal vague preferences which representatives and economic experts can appease through top down policy decisions. No country exemplifies this attitude today better than China, where the single party system of government legitimizes itself by arguing that it is satisfying the population economically and thus any claims by the people for political speech would only disrupt the economic development process. Rancière points out that in the past governments would deny speech to the masses based on the Platonic claim that the people were the stomach who needed to be guided by the head of elite government, but today the governing head 'is unable to distinguish itself from the stomach,' and political speech and opinion is seen as unseemly even for politicians whose job has now become economic administration (Rancière 2010a, 3).

To set up a stage where people can speak and listen to each other rests on the starting assumption that everyone is equal, making the division of society into ordered parts a subject of dispute. Such a statement seems rather benign but underscores the radically different method of politics and anti-politics. Most forms of anti-politics, even ones with benevolent or progressive intent, are distributive in nature and, at best, seek to achieve equality as an outcome. This method paints the individual as a passive recipient who can be satisfied by being handed his or her allocated share. Such individuals can then be acted on as objects of administrative management, parcelled into populations and identity groups who might need more or less. Even the most progressive forms of distributive approaches to government remain anti-political, in that there remains no avenue for the people to construct a stage where they can become actors who are capable of speaking with others on an equal footing. The fact that each individual has a unique opinion, given the basic fact of human plurality, makes a stage for people to express these opinions publicly necessary. To presume that politics can be reduced to distributing and counting shares is to deny plurality and subjectivity.

When politics begins with the presumption of equality, it enables political actors to participate in verifying and testing this presumed equality. This means that political action will seek to assert and extend this presumed equality against any and all material instances of inequality. Arendt associates the movement of participating in political action with freedom, in that she argues freedom appears only with the performance of politics, in the same manner that the drama of a play only appears with its performance (Arendt 2006a, 151). Politics consists in speaking, acting, listening, and creating relationships and associations, activities which leave behind no direct material trace, unlike say an artist who creates a painting. In this sense politics is like other performing arts which require a public space populated by others in order for the art to appear and the virtuosity of the performers to be revealed (Arendt 2006a, 152). Public political space serves as a theatre where people can act, which allows freedom, in the form of political participation, to appear and be exercised.

The freedom of participating in political action relates to the capacity to begin something new. If nothing ever changes, then there is no freedom and thus no capacity to act. Žižek argues that the political act not only changes the symbolic space, but also disturbs the underlying fantasy (Žižek 2008a, 238). In this sense, political action cannot merely be the administrative and legislative activities of modern parliaments, but must allow for the possibility of something truly new and previously unthinkable to come to pass. Žižek's conception of political action fits with Arendt's argument that natality is the central category of the political, as political action is the exercise of freedom, and as such is the capacity to begin something new (Arendt 1998, 9). This newness can seem utterly improbable or even unthinkable before the political event, with the Arab Spring being an example, and in this sense the natality of political participation can change our underlying assumptions about the world.

Political participation as the exercise of freedom and the capacity to initiate the new and unexpected means it is a risky endeavour, which is part of the reason that philosophers have long schemed to control and constrain politics. Given that politics is always conducted among others, to exercise one's freedom to set something new into motion is to take a risk because the beginner can never know what the result will be, due to the intervention of other actors. Given the plurality of people involved in any political act, the shape any action takes gets twisted and turned by numerous people and groups, often leading to outcomes completely contrary to what was originally intended (Arendt 1998, 190). While the people in Egypt were successful in uniting to take down the dictatorship, what came after was unpredictable and, for a good many of these activists, entirely unwanted. The emergence of the military and Islamist groups after the successful removal of Hosni Mubarak speaks to the risk and unpredictable nature of political action. Many conservative commentators warned of these possible outcomes and declared that it was better to stick with Mubarak as dictator than take the risk of removing him, expressing a fundamentally anti-political outlook.[9] All political action must embrace the risk and unpredictability of collective action, because the only alternative is to close off the space of freedom and natality in favour of a controlled and static regime which eliminates politics entirely.

If freedom and change are to be possible, the desire to substitute making for acting in the public sphere must be resisted. Arendt states that 'this attempt to replace acting with making is manifest in the whole body of argument against "democracy," which, the more consistently and better reasoned it is, will turn into an argument against the essentials of politics' (Arendt 1998, 220). In place of collective political action, which presumes the equality of actors and operates by exercising freedom, the model of public affairs based on that of not the actor, dancer, or other performing artist, but of the craftsperson is proposed (Arendt 1998, 225). Politics is reduced to designing blueprints which are meant to be constructed exactly according to design. Such a model of anti-politics replaces the riskiness of political action with a command and obey structure of rulership, eliminating both equality and freedom from the public realm. Today we have accepted this model of rulership and consider it to be legitimate when the rulers are elected, but, as Arendt was always keen to repeat, political freedom means the freedom to participate in politics, or it means nothing at all (Arendt 2006b, 210). To be an actor on the participatory stage of politics means that one is able to debate with equals and to participate in the decisions that affect the wellbeing of the political entity. Choosing one's rulers or executing their designs is hardly a substitute for meaningful participation. Deliberative democracy and direct democracy both fail as participatory alternatives to representation as they do not allow the citizen to participate fully as both decision maker and deliberator, leaving real power outside of the reach of the citizens.

4.3 Participation in an Online Context

While theoretical arguments can be made in favour of the virtues of a more engaged mode of political participation, the practice has always fallen short of the ideal, partly because of the seeming unworkability of most forms of participatory politics. Models of participatory democracy that refer back to the ancient Athenian example are deemed hopelessly utopian and completely unworkable in the context of today's vastly larger pool of citizens. This argument has become commonplace in dismissing the practicality of participatory politics, even among theorists who are otherwise sympathetic (Saco 2002, 35). C.B. MacPherson considered the problem of size to be one of the primary obstacles for participatory democracy, despite his overall enthusiasm for the project of more participation. Macpherson even mused as early as 1977 about using some sort of technological means such as two-way televisions to facilitate more participation but ultimately rules it out for lacking a properly deliberative aspect (MacPherson 1977, 95). The protests of the Arab Spring seemed to hit a similar impasse, as once the unelected dictatorships were overthrown, representative democracy seemed to be the only practical alternative. Even Arendt scholars routinely dismiss her arguments in favour of council democracy as unworkable or utopian (Canovan 1978, 8; Parekh 1981, 171). Despite my enthusiasm for a more participatory politics, these critiques of participatory democracy's practicality are hard to escape. The idea of meeting in councils only seems practical at the micro-level of neighbourhood associations, but anything beyond that small scale would result in insurmountable obstacles in terms of physical distance, space, and time. A form of politics where only ultra-local issues are at stake, however, fails to provide the means for people to engage with the issues they care about. Especially in the context of increasing globalization, restricting one's political energies to micro-local issues seems like a failed attempt to return to some romanticized version of the pre-industrial past.

The lack of clearly workable alternatives to representative democracy has led theorists such as Rancière to simply posit politics as bound up with anti-politics, making political participation only about dissent and protest (Rancière 1999, 31). While these elements must be included in any kind of theory of political participation, to dismiss the ability to take part in decision making is to seriously circumscribe what politics means and what counts as political action. Rather than resort to positing politics as purely oppositional, a new vision of practical participatory politics is necessary, and it is precisely on this point where the internet has the capacity to reinvigorate these debates. As was argued in the chapter on the political realm, concerns of physical distance and time in an online context are not the overwhelming constraints they are in offline space, which allows us to move beyond the primary and most valid criticism of participatory democracy.

Most accounts of how the internet can be beneficial for politics focus on one of three aspects that position the internet in a supporting role. For advocates of representative democracy, the internet becomes another form of communications tool in which candidates use social media and set up websites in order to try to attract more votes. Typical of this approach is the edited volume *The Internet Election*, which analyzes the 2004 United States Presidential election. The internet is treated in terms of its ability to organize supporters and make fundraising efforts more broad based and generally treats the internet as revolutionizing the campaigning process but completely peripheral to the functioning of government (Williams and Tedesco 2006). Even in the context of a comparative study of the internet and national elections done in 2014, there is no mention of using the internet to allow people to actually vote, thus keeping the internet at a safe distance from even the selection of representatives (Kluver et al. 2014). The second method positions the internet as the possible site of a more engaged civic sphere, in which people can deliberate on political issues, and the consensus that results from these deliberations are then meant to guide the decisions of elected leaders. While the deliberative position with respect to the internet is an improvement on the representative position which places the internet on the periphery, deliberative democrats such as Castells,

Dahlberg, and Papacharissi tend to see the internet as a place for a renewed sense of Habermas's bourgeois public sphere, which although it provides more avenues for participating in debate and discussion, it still keeps the internet at arm's length from the actual mechanisms of government (Castells 2007; Papacharissi 2002; Dahlberg and Siapera 2007). Positioning the internet as a site where public space can be built puts me in line with the thinking of many of these theorists, as was outlined in the chapter on the political realm, but in many cases their political theorizing ends at the issue of space and communication. As we know from offline forms of civil society, the fact that it may exist is not enough to bring about any form of sustained democratic participation. The goal is to participate in government, not merely to be able to talk about what the government is doing with other people.

The third model positions the internet as an uncontrolled space of dissent which can formulate the creation of protest movements and help strengthen alternative voices by not needing to rely on traditional forms of corporate-controlled mass media to reach a broad audience (Kahn and Kellner 2004; Howard and Hussain 2013). Kahn and Keller, for instance, accept that the internet is a contested terrain with multiple competing configurations, a point similar to the one being presented here, and as a result 'focus on how oppositional groups and movements use ICTs to promote democracy and social justice on local and global scales' (2004, 5). Like with the other two models of web-enabled democracy, this one again positions the internet as a useful tool that allows activists to create spaces that operate outside of the structures of government. Such an approach which recognizes that the internet is a contested space and rejects the tendency toward totalizing our experiences online is again a significant contribution but falls short of the goal of actually envisioning how a functioning alternative to the status quo might be placed online. While embracing aspects of these models can be useful in formulating a more engaged politics, they essentially skirt the potentially radical impact the internet could have for reinvigorating participatory politics.

Instead of positing the internet as a communications tool, alternative space, or useful supplement, the real potential lies in placing the infrastructure of politics online, and thus reviving aspects of the council system of participation advocated by both Arendt and C.B. Macpherson (1977, 108–109). Instead of accepting the idea that the government and the people must be completely separate entities, the participatory model positions the people as the government in a properly democratic sense. If, however, the stage of politics was not limited to a physical space where only a very select few can actually participate and the audience has little opportunity for input, then the elimination of the gulf between government and citizens could be possible. The only viable means of implementing participatory politics is by placing the stage online. In this sense the internet would alter everything about how politics is conducted, rather than being a mere supplement. People would debate and argue with others online, not just as a means of aggregating interests or creating public sentiments which representatives would act on, but enabling decisions to be made on issues raised directly by the people, not in address to a separate ruling entity but to their fellow citizens.

Placing the political stage online facilitates participation in politics in a number of ways. If one of the most basic elements of political participation is the ability to speak, this capacity becomes much easier online. As was outlined in the chapter on subjectivity, speaking online provides a form of cover for one's personal life, so that the risk of public engagement can be reduced and the likelihood of having speech dismissed on the basis of what someone is, rather than on what they have to say can be reduced. Online speech, in so far as it is actually writing, can facilitate a deeper debate that moves beyond the 'Madison Avenue' methods of electoral campaigns by generating a more substantive focus on the actual issues facing the public (Arendt 2006b, 268). While it is true that the internet can also allow people to publicly state whatever vapid sentiment happens to flutter into their heads, setting up the technology to weed out such comments is not difficult and would obviously be considered when constructing such an online space. Overall the level of political discourse would likely elevate. Currently we have to listen to and consider every thoughtless statement of an elected politician simply because they are the people with decision making authority, while in a more egalitarian online context vapidity is much easier to ignore and tends to be socially punished. Public speech with no content does not stir controversy or provoke debate unless the one issuing such statements is in a position of authority.

Zelda Bronstein points to how taking part in political debate online is not just more convenient but is also emotionally easier (Bronstein 2011, 72). Citing Walter Ong's work on orality, she points to how online debate is easier on the nerves because it lacks the element of 'everyone looking at you at once' that is the case with offline political speech. She also points to Ong's work on how intonation in speech can spur emotions and how certain personalities can dominate others. Offline speeches to an audience are also given from a standing position, which is associated with combativeness and is an aggressive posture, compared to debating online which is done from a weakened seated position (Bronstein 2011, 73). While increasing ease of access, accessibility, and reducing the emotional strain of political participation are, as I have argued, positive benefits of online participation, Bronstein goes on to argue that these conveniences make political participation too easy and that ease of use cheapens the importance of political participation (Bronstein 2011, 73). This argument is related to the elitist argument that will be dealt with later on in this chapter but also relates to a common complaint about slacktivism cheapening issues into clicking a like button or signing an e-petition. Why, however, should political participation be inherently exhausting, emotionally taxing, and all around difficult unless the goal is to constrain participation to only an aristocratic few, whether they be dedicated activists or elected politicians? Bronstein then goes on to argue, citing Turkle's tired argument, that participating online isolates individuals and weakens ties between people (Bronstein 2011, 74). Bronstein's ideal of participation seems to involve small vanguards of dedicated activists rather than broad based movements or the ability for anyone and everyone to easily take part in the political process. In this sense, Bronstein's organizational structure for activists simply mimics the structure of government that she seeks to oppose.

The strength of online participation is precisely the ease of access that critics such as Bronstein do not like. It is simply easier, practically, to allow vast numbers of people to make public statements at the same time, and much easier to read and consider vast numbers of comments posted online than in any offline alternative. Talking verbally and listening aurally are much more consuming of one's attention in the way that reading and writing are not, meaning that an online participatory politics would simply be less time-consuming in general, which would facilitate more participation. Writing and reading also have the advantage over talking and listening of being able to allow for more time to consider what one is writing, and to consider what one is reading. In this sense it can moderate the impact of the angry person with the loud voice demanding to be heard. One can imagine a public assembly where those who yell the loudest become impossible to ignore, while those with calm and reasonable arguments do not get a chance to speak. By placing such speech online and transforming it into written thoughts, the volume of speech becomes much less important than the content. Writing in all capitals in an attempt to convey anger simply does not have the same effect, and is more likely to lead to ridicule than immediate or urgent consideration of what is being hastily conveyed.

Even the much-maligned notion of 'slacktivism,' which often consists of merely liking a Facebook cause or changing a Twitter picture to express solidarity for a cause might have some political potential. Jodi Dean (2009, 22–24) presents a convincing argument that such forms of trivial participation may prevent meaningful participation in that having clicked to a sign a petition or written a blog post that no one will read, we are left feeling like we have made a real contribution and thus participated politically. Such trivial forms of participation, however, may actually serve as a gateway to more sustained political engagements. Christensen finds that online engagement in political activities tended to increase the desire for subjects to participate offline, and that there is no evidence to suggest that slacktivism is replacing more substantial forms of political participation (Christensen 2011). In a thorough study of online and offline political behaviour in the UK, Gibson et al. found that being older, wealthier, male, and white were strong predicators of offline political activity, but that these same groups were not strong predicators of online political activity, demonstrating the internet's capacity to overcome traditional barriers to participation (Gibson, Lusoli, and Ward 2005). A study by Vissers and Stolle of students at McGill University found that political activity online and offline was positively correlated and that those who engaged in Facebook slacktivism were no less likely to participate in other forms of more substantial political engagement (Vissers and Stolle 2014).

Moving beyond concerns of clicktivism or slacktivism, Dean goes on to argue that the internet does provide new avenues for participation but that these avenues have already been captured by anti-political forces (Dean 2009, 17). The most interesting sites on the internet are now driven by user-generated content, as without the participation of users, sites such as YouTube, Facebook, Twitter, or Reddit would sit completely empty of any content. According to Dean, the sites which rely on participation have two anti-political effects. First, they direct people's participatory impulse away from politics and channel it into other means, and second they create an 'intense circulation of content' in which everyone registers an opinion that no one listens to, thus undermining the agonistic and deliberative aspects necessary for politics (Dean 2009, 24). Specifically, Dean cites the example of people having political blogs where they can publicly state their opinions on any given issue whenever they want. The problem, however, is that very few people will read it, and thus people end up feeling like they have participated without their participation being meaningful. Under no circumstances would blogging be considered a model for a new online political realm, and thus Dean's critique, although valid, is hardly a condemnation of online political participation as a whole as she draws her examples from one small element of online activity.

A much more interesting problem is how public relevance algorithms determine the visibility of a post to Reddit or social media. Political theorists need to work with programmers to develop algorithms which ensure the best contribution is the most visible. Much of the dismay with online commenting stems from the fact that visibility is usually not a function of quality, but of popularity or of time. Social websites have algorithms which make socially popular comments the most visible while often newspapers simply do not have any public relevance algorithm and sort comments simply by when they were posted. Dean's concerns can be inverted here, as often the privileging of comments based on time or social popularity lends too much visibility to poorly thought out comments, which can lead people unfamiliar with public relevance algorithms to simply dismiss all online commenting as the lowest form of public discourse possible.

There are plenty of examples of legitimately political uses of the internet today, including Anonymous, the Arab Spring, and the Occupy movement. The real problem with critiquing how people currently use the internet, and then taking this to be a critique of the medium itself, is that it closes off the potential of what the internet could be and how it could be used in the future. The prevailing trend of cyberscepticism has a tendency to downplay or even ignore the potential for politicization that can happen by harnessing the internet, even if it does not rule out such possibilities. In many cases, the cybersceptics make convincing arguments against the old wave of cyberutopians, but it comes off today as a strawman argument. No one believes that internet is going to usher in political change by itself anymore, and by now every internet user knows that they are just as likely to find hotbeds of racism and even post-fascist political movements organizing online as they are to find the seeds of a new form of participatory politics. The fact that the internet is a contested terrain with multiple possible configurations and uses is now somewhat obvious, rendering the cyberutopians and cybersceptics both somewhat archaic. Political theorizing surrounding the internet should be focusing on what can be created and how to push the terrains toward more political participation.

4.4 The Actor and the Audience

Previously I emphasized participation in the form of speech and action and outlined the role of the actor on the political stage. To continue the theatrical metaphor, in order to stage an action, there must be people watching in the audience. Political speech is meaningless if no one hears it, and political action leaves no lasting impact if it is removed from the public eye. A form of politics which is participatory in nature and operates in a similar manner to a theatre can then be said to suffer from the paradox of the theatre. An audience is needed in order to witness the action, while at the same time this audience has tended to be viewed in a negative light, as spectating has traditionally been associated with passivity and inaction, and thus considered to be the opposite of participation (Rancière 2011, 2). What then is the status of those who watch, in the context of a politics that puts such a heavy emphasis on participation and uses theatrical metaphors?

The separation of those who act and those who spectate has led to two significant political responses, albeit both somewhat communitarian in nature. The first response is the most radical, as it rests on simply eliminating the political stage altogether in order to prevent the internal division of the people into those who act and those who spectate. In Plato's critique of poetry, the theatre is a site of illusion and passivity which internally divides the community, sewing disharmony and contradiction (Plato 1991, 603–606). In the *Timaeus*, Plato presents his alternative to the divided theatrical model of politics by presenting a model of community based on the orderly movements of the planets. In this sense Plato eliminates the political stage where some act freely and some spectate in favour of a

> choreographic community, where no one remains a static spectator, where everyone must move in accordance with the community rhythm fixed by mathematical proportion, even if that requires getting old people reluctant to take part in the community dance drunk (Rancière 2011, 5).

This choreographic model has been evident in various totalitarian regimes, from North Korea's mass games, in which over 100,000 people take part in a choreographed gymnastics routine to the hypnotic marching in unison of military parades. By emphasizing collective movement in unison, the harmony of the community can be asserted and there is no room for either the freedom of political movement that goes against the grain or the ability for the spectator to critically reflect on the action she or he witnesses.

Swinging the other way are those who wish to reinvent the political stage altogether rather than abolish it along the lines of Plato's choreographed mass movement. In this sense, there is an attempt to pull everyone into the action of the political drama, thus saving the ideal of the political stage from the problem of the spectator. At its most basic level, this attitude is apparent in the demands for people to vote in elections. The argument goes that if one does not participate in the voting process, then one essentially gives up all claims to active citizenship and must accept radical passivity. The popular version of this sentiment is the common saying that 'if you don't vote, you don't get to complain,' which is paradoxical in itself as it splits the political speech of affirmation and dissent into two separate parts. Central to this argument is the idea that, by voting for a politician, the spectators become part of the process and, thus, are drawn into it as participants, removing the critical distance that may lead to questioning the entire process itself. Even in a representative democracy where participation is constrained to choosing a ruler every couple of years, there is a public demand that the separation between spectator and actor be abolished. In a situation which thrives on public passivity, the dominant ideology is that by going out and voting, the government that is chosen is legitimately made up of the people, and is thus an organ of its wishes and desires. The ideology of representative democracy can then claim there are no rulers and ruled, and no division between spectators and actors.

The demand for audience participation acts as a demand to suspend critical faculties, as when a band that the audience is clearly not enjoying makes a point of trying to exhort the audience members to dance or get involved in the performance. It comes across as an insecure form of trying to prevent judgement. The attempt to eliminate spectators and their critical distance is evident as well in communitarian attempts to posit community as an organizing principle. To become part of the community and remove oneself from one's critical distance from it functions as an attempt to remove the possibility of an outside that can criticize, or as Rancière calls it, 'a part with no part'. Instead of either of these communitarian attempts to abolish the division between spectator and actor, political emancipation can operate in the manner of an emancipated theatre, where, rather than trying to eliminate the spectators, the boundaries between those who look and those who act can be traversed (Rancière 2011, 19).

The problem with the supposed paradox of the spectator lies in the idea that listening and watching are passive and, therefore, not only the opposite of action but that acting and watching are mutually exclusive. In reality, listening is part of the acting and speaking process, and the difference between them is not as evident or even existent as the critics of the passive audience think. Part of being a good speaker is being a good listener, and to be a good actor one must take into consideration those with whom one is acting in concert.

As Derek Barker argues, this is the fundamental lesson of Sophocles' *Antigone*. Speech and action in isolation are disastrous, and being a good citizen means being willing to listen to and engage with others (Barker 2009, 38). Creon and Antigone both speak and act without listening to the other, while Haemon listens to both and grows into a mature citizen. Political speech as a series of disconnected monologues fails to have any impact in the same way as attempting to start a revolution or protest in isolation from other people is futile. The collective and performative nature of politics demands that not just other actors be included, but spectators as well. Spectators who observe, draw connections, make judgements and develop their own interpretations from what they have seen.

The spectator, far from being removed from political participation, is the one who engages in the most critical political faculty of all, namely judgement (Arendt 1981, 192–193). The political spectator is like the theatrical spectator, not someone sitting passive and agape before a spectacle who needs to be motivated into action. Given that action is less common, watching should be conceived of as our normal condition of being (Rancière 2011, 17). We watch, we draw connections, and we judge. Given that so much of politics depends on the clash of different opinions and the presentation of unique perspectives, the role of judging is all the more important. Every political decision involves the presentation of multiple choices without any objectively true solution which could be discovered through scientific principles. Politics is like one's taste in music or film. It comes down to a matter of subjective judgements. In this sense, the judgemental audience is at least as important a form of political participation as the speeches and actions which happen on the stage of action. A participatory politics open to everyone means that an actor must sit down and listen as a spectator, and that there must be no barrier that prevents anyone in the audience from standing up and getting onto the stage. The separation of spectator and actor is preserved, but there is no rigid barrier preventing people from crossing from audience to actor and actor to audience and spectating is considered just as important as acting.

Participating in politics online can also help lower the wall between spectator and actor. In-person debates take the form of one person speaking and everyone else listening, which has the effect of clearly separating the spectator from the actor. In an online context, however, there need not be an unsurmountable wall of separation between speakers and listeners, because when reading people's comments one can also comment and reply at the same time. There is no need to take turns in a rigidly delineated manner between only spectating and only acting. Spectators can more easily be empowered to engage in judgement, as mechanisms can be set up where, upon reading a comment, a reader can click an agree or disagree button to register their judgement without having to write out a comment outlining their own position. Given that most people in online forums are 'lurkers,' or people who often read but do not post to discussion forums, to be able to share their judgement publicly without having to type out a comment is empowering (Nonnecke and Preece 1999). Spectators can become the drivers of what issues are important in this way, as their quiet judgements will drive what issues get noticed and discussed. This is significant because in an offline context it is usually only the actors who are willing to speak who drive the conversation, as there is very little recourse for the spectator to push the conversation or debate in another direction without directly speaking out. Online participation can greatly empower the spectator and, thus, make the content of politics more reflective of what the average citizen is concerned with, rather than being reflective only of what the most outspoken citizens wish to discuss.

It is important to blur the line between spectator and actor without actually abolishing it. Some critics of participatory websites point to the fact that almost all content that is created on a site such as Wikipedia for instance, is performed by a very select few, and most people simply read the articles without ever editing them (Polletta 2013, 43). Rather than trying to salvage the participatory aspect by claiming that we need to change how we conceive of equality, as Polletta argues, we simply need to realize that spectatorship is not 'worse' than participation but tied to it. The fact that not everyone edits Wikipedia does not make it less participatory or make it into some kind of new structure of exclusionary elitism as some critics have claimed (Kittur et al. 2007). If everyone was forced to write or edit a Wikipedia article in order to read one, not only would readership vastly decline, but the quality of content posted would also decline. Spectatorship and action go hand in hand and require each other. The fact that some may not feel the need to act most of the time is not a problem, especially in an online context where spectators can be emancipated in the way described by Rancière (2011).

By placing the activities of politics related to its communicative and decision making aspects online, a whole host of new forms of participation open up. There are a plethora of possibilities of how such a political stage could operate, as well as many possible different implementations that could come about. Many existing websites provide nascent possibilities which could serve as inspiration for the creation of an online political infrastructure. While social media sites are problematic because of their social nature, one could imagine networks of people connected not by social ties but around political issues. Instead of becoming friends with another person, one could join an issue, immediately linking with other potential actors who could be rallied to transform debates into actions that rearrange the world. Discussion forums such as Reddit, which are driven by users submitting links which can be upvoted or downvoted based on how interesting they are, could serve as a model for deciding which issues were of higher priority within a political community. The discussion aspect of sites like Reddit could also serve as the basis for debate on popular issues, as it allows people to respond directly to others and upvote or downvote individual comments.

While Reddit's aim with the upvote and downvote system was to weed out and hide irrelevant comments, in more politically oriented subforums, this system breaks. Unpopular opinions get downvoted as a form of disagreement, which is politically problematic as the Reddit public relevance algorithm automatically hides comments with a negative voting score. In a properly political forum unpopular opinions need the same visibility as popular ones. Different methods and algorithms would have to be developed which send not just the most popular opinions to the top, but also the most unpopular, the most controversial, and the ones which provoked the most replies. There are many examples of nascent possibilities that could be transformed to facilitate politics, but too many critics of online participation simply look at the flaws, such as Reddit's downvote system hiding unpopular political opinions, and then deem the internet as a whole unsuitable to politics.[10] What is needed is some creative thinking about how the internet could be used as a political stage, rather than dismissing it based on certain flawed websites which were not meant to be used for political purposes in the first place. Due to the malleability of the software, new sites with new mechanics and algorithms could easily be programmed. Too often people without programming experience have a tendency to treat the internet as simply a static given, and not as a place where new spaces and experiences can be created.

4.5 The Elitist Argument against Participation: Too Much Quantity Degrades Quality

Beyond the space and time argument, which the internet renders invalid, the most serious argument against participatory politics has to do with the quality and quantity of the participation. This argument takes two forms; the elitist version argues that the quantity of participation will overwhelm the quality while the populist argument argues that the quality of participation will overwhelm the quantity. Both versions would seem to be amplified when considering online participation, however, as I will show, online participation can more than compensate for any increase in negative aspects to which these two critiques point. This section will deal with the elitist version of the quality versus quantity argument, while the next section will look at the populist version of it.

In its most simple form, the elitist argument states that by allowing anyone and everyone to participate politically it will lead to poor decisions and the consideration of uninformed and unreasonable opinions. The ultimate fear is that the unwashed masses will degrade politics into some sort of vulgar talk show where people scream their prejudices at each other and nothing serious can happen. The elitist argument is persistent in the history of political philosophy, as it begins with Plato's philosopher kings and is even raised against representative democracy by the likes of John Stuart Mill who argued that the educated elite should be given two votes in elections to compensate for the enfranchisement of the working class (Miller 2010, 182). Remnants of this suspicion toward the political intelligence of the average person persist in institutions such as the Canadian Senate and British House of Lords, which were originally meant to operate as a check on any potential 'democratic excess' that might occur as a result of allowing regular people to choose their own representatives for the House of Commons.

The elitist argument becomes amplified in the online context, as there is a persistent view that allowing just anyone to publicly comment on a news story, for example, simply leads to a series of vacuous and pointless comments. Often the toxicity of online commenting is blamed on anonymity and the so-called 'internet disinhibition effect' (Suler 2004), but there is no reason to believe that someone would only make a ridiculous comment online when he or she would otherwise never make the same comment when discussing the same news article with friends. Anonymity does not cause people to act immaturely but allows them to reveal what they really think without worry of social consequences. Anonymity breeds honesty, whereas social pressures may lead individuals to make insincere political comments in the name of fitting into one's social context. Online commentary on political issues tends to cover a wider spectrum of beliefs, including ones that are generally not socially acceptable, not because anonymity makes people act differently, but because it enables honesty.

A second aspect to the perception that online discussion is of lower quality relates to its publicity. Traditionally the revealing of opinions, including ones which are ignorant or prejudiced, are kept to a small group of people due to the lack of a public political stage. The difference between talking about politics online and among a small group of people is not a matter of anonymity but is a matter of how many people can see the comments. The founder of Gawker, one of the larger websites which focus on allowing users to comment on posted articles, argues that the site may move toward a model where only a select few pre-approved readers will be allowed to comment on any given story, in an attempt to improve the quality of comments on the site (Gross 2012). The real issue, however, of why people are either so willing to engage in toxic behaviour, post pointless comments, or proudly proclaim their ignorance publicly is not merely a matter of the functioning of the internet but poses the question of why are these people so uninformed and poorly behaved in the first place? The argument for the internet disinhibition effect rests on the assumption that in offline space the same people who act boorish online would be capable of serious and reasonable political debate offline. In contrast to Suler's initial argument, psychological research is increasingly demonstrating that people who behave badly online tend to also behave badly offline (Buckels, Trapnell, and Paulhus 2014). In this sense, the internet does not turn people into miscreants; it simply makes people's normal behaviour more visible to a wider audience.

The elitist argument looks at some of the worst examples of poor behaviour and uninformed political discourse online and then draws the conclusion that most people are incapable of serious political activity or at least that the majority lack the education necessary to take part politically. This argument, however, confuses cause and effect. In a system where the vast majority are alienated from participation there is no motivation to become informed and knowledge-able about either the political system or any given daily issue. Politicians debate and decide on these issues, not the average person. Thus, when comments are solicited from the public on news stories for example, is it really surprising that a good deal of them come off as ignorant or vapid? If people were given a real opportunity to participate, the motivation to get informed becomes stronger, especially if one's opinions will be tested in debate by others who are highly knowledgeable and educated on the topic. To continue with the metaphor of the theatre, can one expect a good performance out of an actor who has never had any practice acting, never had any education as an actor, and has never been on stage before? Clearly not, but the elitist argument essentially attempts to naturalize the lack of opportunity into a lack of natural ability.

The idea that participation spurs people to become more informed seems to fly in the face of the claims that internet commenting is the bottom of the barrel when it comes to serious discourse. Especially among journalists there is a common theme that enabling mass participation through the internet simply brings out the worst in people (Smith 2011). The quality of commenting, however, depends on which sites are analyzed and the algorithmic structure of the commenting system. The majority of news sites whose primary medium is offline, operate on a flat commenting model in which the original story is posted with an unconnected list of unrelated comments responding directly to the original article. This is a problematic algorithm for dealing with comment visibility, as users are unable to reply and debate with each other while the list tends to simply be sorted by when a comment was posted. These sites lack a public relevance algorithm which helps sort through the deluge of comments and gives higher visibility to more interesting and relevant comments. By contrast, the nested tree structure of Reddit enables users to have back and forth debates and discussions which are easy for readers to follow. The situation of the newspaper comments is precisely what Jodi Dean critiques as talk without listening, as on such sites there is no formation of relationships (either friendly or adversarial) among users, because they do not talk to each other. Most comments on Canadian news sites have a tendency to be directly aimed at the article or are sometimes even addressed to the Prime Minister, rather than fellow commenters. In this sense, the newspaper commenting sections mirror the structure of government and citizen, where the government makes the decisions and the best the citizen can do is yell in protest. The structure of authority is maintained where the commenters are alienated, taking on the role of yelling into an unresponsive void. The journalist (or the person who posted the story off a news wire service) rarely responds to comments on an article, just as the government rarely engages in debate with individual citizens. With this structure it is no wonder that newspaper comment sections seem to bring out the worst in people and fail to generate any interesting discussion.

The fundamental problem with the structure of most newspaper comments sections, contributing to their poor quality, is the lack of interaction and debate between users. When someone says something toxic, there is no real way to engage with or challenge that person directly. Comment replies get lost in the flat list, or if there is some nested structure, the original commenter rarely sees it. If one can get away with saying anything without challenge, then this will naturally lead to more vacuous and toxic comments. On sites which are structured toward commenting and not simply talking at the original article, such as Reddit, there tends to be a much higher level of discourse. On Reddit you cannot help but notice when people think your comment is of low quality, due to the fact each comment gets a score from voting and replies are sent directly to you as messages. Posting a low quality comment on a newspaper website, by contrast, will not lead to any awareness that it might be of poor quality.

Some newspaper websites have attempted to combat toxicity in the comment section by requiring users to register their real names and even to link their comments to a Facebook account. One of the most notorious news commenting websites in Canada was the now defunct Sun News Network which required a Facebook link with real names for all comments. Despite this real name policy, Sun News had a reputation for having one of the most toxic commenting communities in the Canadian media landscape. Comments on that site tended to be overly personal and insulting since a user could easily click through to a commenter's Facebook page to gather some personal information in order to craft a particularly personalized insult. Real names policies and linking comments to a person's offline identity do not create more accountability which leads to higher quality comments but, in fact, simply provides more ammunition for character attacks which can become more personalized and thus more hurtful. By contrast, Reddit's structure promotes engagement among users who are able to police each other through critical debate and downvoting poor quality comments. In this sense, the disinhibition effect which leads to the posting of poor quality comments is not a result of internet anonymity but a result of being able to talk without reply. When everything one says is subject to critical response, one becomes more careful in what one says, and there is a strong motivation to do a little research to make sure one's statements have some kind of factual backing. Seeing that one's comment has received hundreds of downvotes and generated tens of critical replies demonstrating how one is wrong is embarrassing and provides social impetus to do better next time by becoming more informed on the issue.

Contrary to the elitist fear that mass participation will degrade political discourse, making participation more open and accessible could very well empower common sense. The current system enables lobbying by interest groups, and if they are motivated enough or have enough money, they can easily sway policy in their favour even if their demands run contrary to the public interest or even common sense. Industry lobbying of government would be muted in a more participatory political system. It would be more difficult for a lobbyist to persuade the public to do things that go against its interest, as compared to convincing a few politicians. There is also the issue of small but motivated groups who rely on the lack of engagement by the public to get measures passed. A good example are the conspiracy-oriented anti-fluoride movement and anti-wind farm movements in Ontario (Krishnan 2013; Martin 2013). Both groups rely on arguments that are scientifically unsupported and which, when faced with broader public scrutiny, tend to be ridiculed as pseudoscience. When anti-fluoride groups show up to every city council meeting and demand that their issue be discussed, it can make it seem like that issue is disproportionately important to the public. Very few people have the motivation to show up at a public meeting to counter the claims of anti-wind farm or anti-fluoride activists because, to most people, defending common sense is hardly something that inspires political passion. The lack of visible opposition, however, is what allows these measures to get passed. In a participatory system, such issues would face much broader public rebuke and be quickly pushed aside in favour of more serious considerations. The ease of posting a rebuttal online can elevate political discourse and minimize the effect of those who rely on not being publicly challenged to push their issue.

Once one accepts that the elitist argument against mass participation lacks merit, an inevitable corollary is the question about having the time to decide and debate every minute detail of every issue and proposal. This question seems to derive from the attitude that voting in elections is a civic duty. Thus, in a participatory democracy, it is assumed there would be a duty to participate in every possible debate and decision. There would, however, be little incentive or need to be involved in every issue. People would naturally only gravitate toward participating in issues that mattered to them, and in fact it would amount to interference to try to join the decision on every issue. It is always better to not participate than to participate blindly, and there will be a measure of self-selection on any given political issue. At the same time, if someone simply was not interested in politics that person would be free to let others make the decisions, allowing the pursuit of wealth accumulation or whatever else one might prefer to political participation. Participation could take on a number of different roles, ranging from complete uninvolvement, to only voting on final proposals, to debating the crafting of proposals, to discussing issues which the political body should be addressing. The fact that participation would be a matter of self-selection leads into the flip-side of the quantity versus quality argument: namely, that these self-chosen people will form a new elite which would undermine democratic participation.

4.6 The Populist Argument against Participation: Too Much Quality Degrades Quantity

The populist argument against participation states that if too much emphasis is placed on the quality of political discourse and participation, the citizens who self-select to participate will form a new elite which will push out most people and, thus, not actually increase participation at all. Hindman makes this argument with relation to blogs, arguing that the internet does not democratize the media but simply transfers power to another form of elite, thus reproducing a structure of elite driven politics online (Hindman 2008, 102). The problem with an elite-driven politics is not, however, simply a matter of how many are participating. The real problem with an elite-based politics derives from the fact that becoming a member of the elite-few able to participate is not a matter of self-selection (Arendt 2006b, 271). Non-participation in the context of a self-selected elite would be a personal choice, making it fundamentally different from representative democracy in which the exclusion from participation is not up to the individual. The ability to self-exclude from politics also ensures that the negative liberty of being free from politics is upheld (Arendt 2006b, 272). Thus, even if a small number of citizens end up as the major participators, it would still be more participatory, because it would allow those who most want to participate to do so, and allow those with no interest in politics to go about their private business without demands that voting is a civic duty and the associated guilt trips.

Having only a small number of self-chosen participants is not problematic, because anyone can choose to become part of that small group of participants meaning that there are no barriers to enter the public realm like there are under representative systems. If one does not like how a participatory self-selected elite is doing things, then one can simply join it in order to try to change how things are done. Ironically this tends to be the argument used in favour of representative democracy, in which if one does not like the government, one simply needs to run for office and join it. Of course, winning office is an extremely difficult task, as it relies on being selected by others and is not simply a personal choice as it would be in a participatory democracy. On another level, even if a self-selected elite is not such a bad thing, the probability of this occurring should be questioned as well. While research on preliminary online participatory experiments shows that very few people participated, such experiments were also relatively limited in scope (Saglie and Vabo 2009; Dahlberg 2001a). As the ability to influence public decisions grow, the number of people interested in participating would in all likelihood grow as well. The number of participants, however, is not a measure of legitimacy in a participatory system because participation is not closed off and, thus, the self-chosen participants do not need to try to legitimize their authority with an appeal to broad support, such as in a representative system. It is on this issue where the major difference between Arendt and Macpherson's participatory models can be detected. Macpherson still thinks in terms of legitimacy being derived from the number of participants, and thus poses general apathy as a potential problem for participatory democracy (1977, 111). However, if everyone is going to be participating in everything, it will inevitably lead to less democratic outcomes as it would encourage uninformed participation. Less people participating without barrier to entry is always more democratic than more people participating just for the sake of participating. Understanding this idea that less participation may actually be more democratic may sound counter-intuitive but requires overcoming the ideology of legitimacy that only makes sense within an elite-driven representative democracy.

The use of the internet can vastly simplify participation and, thus, make participation more accessible. One no longer needs to have a household full of slaves in order to be afforded the time to enter the public arena, as in ancient Athens. The increased proliferation and penetration of the internet through not just computers but mobile phones makes participation easy and accessible. Even someone who works long hours could receive cell phone alerts about issues he or she was following, which would keep people informed without having to travel somewhere and dedicate a specific period of time to political activities. At the same time, cheap mobile devices with internet connectivity are rapidly spreading across the developing world while public libraries with internet terminals can facilitate access to the political realm by even the most marginalized sectors of the population. In fact, there may even be a reverse bias in political participation in which those with time-consuming professional jobs, who are today the most likely to become politicians due to their wealth, actually participate less because their occupations take up so much of their time. The tendency for a participatory politics to be dominated by educated professionals or business elites would be offset by those able to dedicate more time to political matters.

Another way of dealing with the populist argument that politics would simply be taken over by a new elite relates to the notion of public happiness and the experience of freedom which comes from political activity. Currently, politics is treated as a kind of burden that usually wealthy people must grudgingly enter into, in order to preserve their ability to accumulate private wealth. This attitude is the modern version of Plato's argument that the philosopher must trudge back into the cave and rule the city in order to make it safe for philosophy, which was then modified by Locke into the burden of property owners to ensure their property is kept safe. Participatory politics emphasizes the public element of public affairs and affirms participating in the decisions and debates of one's community as empowering. Rather than viewing participation as an annoying burden necessary to promote private wealth, political participation should be reoriented as a means to facilitate public happiness. It is the loss of the concept of public happiness as participation in politics that Arendt is most critical of when it comes to the modern revolutions which she otherwise admired. She finishes *On Revolution* by paraphrasing Sophocles and arguing that 'it was the *polis*, the space of men's free deeds and living words, which could endow life with splendour' and thus make life's burden bearable (Arendt 2006b, 273). Given the opportunity to actually participate, many people would discover the joys of political participation, which would have the dual effect of making those who self-choose to engage in politics be primarily concerned with the public good over private advantage, as well as be less likely to form into a rigid elite with a common background, economic status, or education simply because self-empowerment is something universally desirable.

One final aspect of the quantity versus quality argument which should be considered is a hybrid version of the elite and populist argument developed by Mark Warren, a prominent advocate of deliberative democracy. Warren argues that modern society is simply much too complex to allow for citizen participation, as people would simply be in way over their heads when it comes to working out the complex issues that face contemporary societies. He argues that participatory politics would in fact turn into a technocratic situation where only specialists could participate in any meaningful way, thus alienating the vast majority. He proposes to fix this problem through a deliberative model in which citizens have spaces outside of the formal institutions of the state to form opinions (Warren 1996). If society is so complex that only experts can engage in proper political action, then why do we have elections to choose our political leaders today? Deliberative democracy generally places a layer between the state and the people, and, by engaging in this civil society, the public can develop informed and rational opinions which are supposed to guide the decisions of politicians. If the public, however, are limited to more general discussions of the issues because of their complexity, what guarantee is there that an elected government will have any more expertise than the general population? Very rarely are experts in their fields elected to parliaments. So what happens when the elected politicians fail to acknowledge the complexity of contemporary society because they themselves lack expertise? Is it better to hope that elected politicians will listen to scientists on matters such as the causes of climate change, or is it better to let those scientists participate directly?

The problem with the complexity argument is that it assumes expertise from existing politicians or, at least, assumes that they will defer to experts on matters of fact and will defer to civil society on matters of opinion. Neither of these assumptions holds under representative democracy, and deliberative democracy is at best a mild modification of it. There is overwhelming scientific consensus that human activity is causing climate change, and yet little is being done to address climate change even in countries where public opinion matches scientific fact. By allowing experts in their fields to directly participate in politics, they can help inform and shape the debate on complex issues that require specialized knowledge. If today's political issues are more complex, then, if anything, this is an argument to get more people involved. The likelihood of a small group of elected politicians making informed decisions outside their realm of speciality (or contrary to their private business interests) is much less likely than in a situation where participants (including specialists) were self-chosen. In addition, there is no reason to believe that citizens would necessarily need to participate in every single detail of crafting policy or be engaged in every aspect of a public project. If a political body decided that a bridge needed to be built, it obviously would not be debating and voting on every last detail of its construction and architecture and would leave that up to engineers and technical experts. Everyone would not need to be an expert in everything, just as today's politicians are not.

The recent surge in protests across the world demonstrates that there is a latent frustration with governments that fail to provide avenues of meaningful participation. As the internet increases the ability for people to participate in all aspects of life, from media and entertainment to politics, the old argument that there is not enough time and space for participatory politics is losing its lustre. By placing the infrastructure of politics online, participation on a wide scale is fully realizable and can provide citizens with the opportunity to exercise their freedom to speak and act politically. Politics is performative in nature, and can be likened to a theatrical performance, as it requires spectators to witness and remember the action. These spectators are not merely passive onlookers, but engage in critical judgement of what they see. Representative democracy tends to cast out the spectators and transform them into easily swayed consumers. An online participatory politics would soften the barrier between spectator and actor as the role of the spectator would be magnified through the ease of registering judgements. Online participation would remove barriers to entry, but would not be premised on the idea that everyone would need to participate in every decision. Self-selection would be an important factor in ensuring that debates were informed and relevant and help ward off the fear that such a democratic politics would lead to ignorant decisions.

If participatory politics can be likened to a theatrical performance, then it has the most in common with a tragedy. The desire to participate usually stems from disagreement and conflicting opinions. Individuals want to offer their opinions because they are unique and different from others, which brings them into conflict with their peers. The next chapter will develop the idea that politics, like a tragedy, is about participating in conflicts and disagreements on political issues, rather than trying to develop a society where all conflict is reconciled. The continued existence of conflict is necessary if politics is to remain participatory. If all conflict disappeared, then what would political participants have left to do?

CHAPTER 5

Conflict

5.1 Agonism and Antagonism

Returning to the picture developed in the previous chapters, politics so far consists of a plurality of unique subjects participating in meaningful speech and action inside of an online political realm. Given that these subjects are unique, it is inevitable that political participation will be driven by disagreement. The procedure of politics is a means to sort out disputes, which is a common point of agreement among advocates of representative democracy, deliberative democracy, and the participatory agonistic democracy being advanced here. Politics is predicated on using speech to talk through these disputes and arrive at a decision, rather than using violent force to impose a decision (Arendt 1998, 26). The nature of these disputes is, however, highly contested. Representative democracy advocates an economic model of interest aggregation, in which voters express preferences via competitive elections, enabling these representatives to then make the decisions. Disputes on issues are displaced into a competition for offices among parties, a model Joseph Schumpeter accurately labelled as 'competitive elitism' (Schumpeter 1994). Deliberative democrats, such as Habermas and Rawls, posit disagreement as an institutional flaw which can be solved by better institutions. Disputes are merely a matter of temporary miscommunication which, through rational deliberation, can be solved in a way such that all parties involved can be satisfied with the outcome.

Against these two approaches, agonistic pluralism seeks to assert the ineradicability of political disagreement and conflict, and celebrates it as what gives politics its reason for being. The agonistic approach has its roots in thinkers as diverse as Machiavelli, Nietzsche, and Arendt, and finds contemporary expression in the work of Chantal Mouffe, Bonnie Honig, and to some extent Jacques Rancière. Agonistic pluralism recognizes that plurality brings conflict and that the best way to deal with such conflicts is to allow them to find political

---

How to cite this book chapter:

Smith, T. G. 2017. *Politicizing Digital Space: Theory, The Internet, and Renewing Democracy.* Pp. 99–121. London: University of Westminster Press. DOI: https://doi.org/10.16997/book5.e. License: CC-BY-NC-ND 4.0

expression. The goal of politics is to treat those who disagree as political adversaries to be persuaded through political speech, rather than as enemies to be eliminated (Mouffe 2009, 103). Politics is not a matter of antagonistic friends and enemies, as Carl Schmitt would have it, but of agonistic adversaries. Agonistic adversaries do not patronizingly tolerate the position of others or simply ignore those who disagree, but instead actively critique and debate each other.

Agonistic pluralism presents a middle ground on the status of disagreement and conflict. By taming antagonism into a political contest it prevents the extremes of both Schmittian ultrapolitics, which posits violence as constantly present, and the conflict-eliminating assertion of consensus found in deliberative democracy. Both extremes are anti-political, as dissent is radically expelled. For Schmitt, the enemy cannot be debated or persuaded because they are foreign and lack a common ground. Politics is between states for Schmitt, and enemies are those who must be driven back inside their own borders (Schmitt 2007, 36). For deliberative democrats, the answer to the extreme forms of antagonism pointed to by Schmitt is often the radical negation of conflict through the desire to bring about consensus.

Against both of these extreme positions on conflict, the goal of democracy should not be to eliminate 'we/they distinctions' altogether, but to make it so that these political distinctions are compatible with pluralism (Mouffe 2005, 14). In this way, Mouffe and the other agonistic theorists present a middle ground on conflict which retains the value of political disagreement against both the consensual attempt to generate total agreement through communicative rationality and the violent negation of conflict through the use of force which is always present in the Schmittian conception of politics. Consensus and violence, however, tend to operate not as extreme opposite poles, but instead circle into each other. When there is no political way to express dissent, violence can become an option. At the same time, the violent suppression of conflict is always an imposition of conflict-negating consensus.

An agonistic form of politics which embraces disagreement means that the persistence of conflict is of benefit to this approach, rather than a drawback as the deliberative democrats argue (Erman 2009). Politics is fundamentally about making decisions on conflicting courses of action, in which there is no objective or rationally discoverable ideal solution (Mouffe 2005, 110). By ensuring that the political realm is a site of agonistic contest and disagreement, political outlets are provided which channel antagonisms into non-violent political agonisms. Lacking a political outlet for such disagreements, conflict can become antagonistic and turn into a matter of moral absolutes or a conflict between identities rather than ideas (Mouffe 2009, 104). Rather than political adversaries who need to be persuaded through speech, those who disagree get cast as morally evil or radically other in which they become enemies to be destroyed (Mouffe 2005, 15). When people lack the outlet to articulate their dissent politically because of the imposition of consensus, then those political disagreements will find expression in another form. Put in Lacanian terms, when the symbolic of political speech is foreclosed, the disagreement will return in the real, in the guise of racism, sexism, or extremist religious movements (Žižek 2008a, 237).

The upsurge in xenophobic far right wing political parties in Europe and the upswing in fundamentalist religious movements across the world are examples of how conflicts which lack a means to be articulated politically can turn into violent antagonisms (Mouffe 2005, 66–72; Žižek 2008a, 250–257). One of the most striking examples is the rise of the British National Party in the context of the morphing of the British Labour Party into New Labour under Tony Blair. While Labour traditionally represented the economic interests of the predominantly white working class, the abandonment of social democratic principles and the adoption of neoliberalism by New Labour fundamentally alienated a large section of the working class. Lacking a social democratic discourse which critiqued the more excessive aspects of neoliberal capitalism, sections of the British working class felt politically abandoned and turned to the only other societal critique of their lower economic position that was being publicly presented: that of the British National Party. The BNP presented the argument that the white working class was poor because of immigrants destroying the social fabric of Great Britain, thus channeling a critique of political economy into essentialist racial antagonism. The same phenomena could be seen across the Middle East prior to the Arab Spring movement. Lacking any political critiques of neoliberal capitalism in the post-Cold War era, the only opposition came from Islamist groups who were able to transmute political and economic discontent into an argument about the moral decay of secular society and the need to re-embrace religion (Prashad 2007, 260–275).

The rise of these extremist groups is directly related to the lack of political outlet for people to express their discontent and open up a conflict. If people feel there is something wrong but are unable to express this sentiment in political terms because politics is closed off due to the imposition of consensus, it is no wonder that people will support any sort of group willing to present a conflict, even if it is on racist or fundamentalist grounds. This is part of the appeal of these extremist groups. They break the mainstream consensus and call for clear cut decisions to be made which will generate winners and losers (Rancière 2010a, 89). Rather than presenting a vague and technocratic approach where core issues are not up for debate, these groups are willing to open a conflict and take a clear position. Their extreme positions are not political, however, as they tend to be merely an expression of Schmittian internal consensus, in which opening a conflict with an external enemy for the purposes of pushing them out is meant to bring about an internal harmony which restores consensus.

While extremist groups are the more problematic expression of the lack of ability to translate social antagonisms into political agonisms, the same issue occurs within representative government. Since it has become a popular cliché to claim that politics, referring to representative government, has become too divisive and conflictual, how does this fit within the framework of agonistic pluralism which presents representative government as anti-political? The bulk of what people do not like about politicians, and which they label as conflict, is not a vigorous clash of ideas but bickering over trivial differences motivated by party affiliation. This form of partisan-driven conflict without any real disagreement or debate of real issues is the very definition of consensus, the 'state of the world in which everyone converges in veritable worship of the little difference, in which strong passions and great ideals yield to the adjustments of narcissistic satisfactions' (Rancière 2010a). The primary example of this sort of consensual system where irrelevancies are elevated to the status of alleged great divides is the United States, which in the popular and some academic literature, is posited as deeply divided between Republicans and Democrats with fundamentally different visions for the country. In reality the two parties are virtually identical in policy and there is next to no debate on big ideas. The illusion of political conflict, which is derived from having two teams both wanting to win but not having any significant ideological differences, is extremely powerful at papering over the actual lack of serious debate and political conflict, as people get swept up in cheering for their team.

In this sense, the conflict that derives from individuals and parties competing for office who essentially agree can be much more bitter and divisive than actual political conflict. If one cannot criticize the opinions and views of one's political opponent, because they are for the most part very similar to one's own, the only other avenue is an attack on character. The more elections and party politics move toward a consensual neoliberal position, the more elections have become personal and bitter. The wish to overcome the pettiness of personal attacks and dirty tricks takes on a consensual guise, with calls to overcome conflict. The people who see electoral democracy as too divisive and filled with petty insults should advocate not for yet more consensus which caused the problem in the first place, but for the expression of real conflict, so that politics can have substance, alleviating the need to devolve into character assassination. In addition to misidentifying the nature of political conflict and confusing it with personal insult, the advocates of consensus fail to take into consideration the many positive effects that political conflict generates. Disagreement need not be an unfortunate reality that we begrudgingly deal with through debate and political decision, but can lead to personal empowerment and a wider consideration for others. The ability to engage in a conflict of opinions does not degrade politics into petty insults but, as we will see, can actually increase the overall level of civility.

5.2 Consensus as Exclusion

The problem with the deliberative democracy approach is that it fails to recognize that consensus and plurality are incompatible. All consensus on political matters is always the expression of a hegemony and thus generates exclusion. When applied, consensual decision making does not work by including all possible perspectives but by radically eliminating them. It becomes a means for denying dissent altogether rather than generating consensual compromises. The consensual elimination of conflict has two responses to persistent dissent: forcing everyone into the consensual whole or radically excluding dissenters. The first method follows Rousseau and argues that dissenters must be forcefully compelled to agree, or be 'forced to be free' as he puts it (Rousseau 2003, 11). Dissent and the conflict it generates are positioned as obstacles to political freedom in this sense, rather than the proper exercise of it, causing this brand of consensus to veer toward totalitarianism. It becomes not enough for even an overwhelming majority to agree on a proposal, but every single person must make a declaration of public agreement. The door to a police state which is concerned with monitoring how people think is kicked wide open in this scenario.

Even at the relatively smaller scale of activist movements, such as Occupy Wall Street or the alterglobalization movement, issues of dissent and coercion in relation to consensus-based decision making procedures are apparent. In many of the smaller organizational meetings associated with these movements there becomes an overwhelming social pressure to simply give in to the consensus opinion and not state one's own disagreements. If someone has an irreconcilable disagreement against the majority, they act to simply block the process from moving forward since they must be made to agree in order for the decision to be considered resolved.[11] This provides a motivation to simply feign agreement for the sake of moving things along, which naturally leads to later resentment and is likely part of the reason why activist groups so often shatter and splinter into new factions in such dramatic fashion. If proposals were the subject of a vote after a debate which played out all the disagreements, a decision could be made which preserved the ability for those who disagreed to express and maintain their disagreement, while still moving on to making a decision if the majority agreed (Biehl and Bookchin 1998, 60–61). Potentially even worse, dissenters against a consensus may be asked to simply 'stand aside' on the issue under consideration in order to move things along, but this 'nullifies the dissenter as a political being. It resolves the problem of dissent essentially by removing the dissenter from the political sphere and eliminating the dissenting view from the forum of ideas' (Biehl and Bookchin 1998, 61). Without a mechanism to vote, disagreement is radically quashed and there becomes an overwhelming social pressure from the other members of the group to simply go along with the herd and not be obstructionist. People with strong personalities tend to become the de facto leaders in such a situation, where those with quieter personalities are less inclined to speak up if they have no simple mechanism of registering disagreement. Hierarchies can thus form based purely on personality types and social pressures. The ability to register individual dissent while assenting to the wishes of the majority is much healthier for group cohesion than forcing people to publicly state consent to things they fundamentally disagree with or kicking them out of the group altogether.

While forcing people to agree to proposals they do not actually accept is extremely problematic, the other option is to disqualify people as political subjects for disagreeing. This is the reality of consensus, namely, that it is always based on an exclusion (Mouffe 2005, 11). The consensus system rests on the idea that the whole is whole and the nothing is nothing and that there cannot be any part with no part leftover which can open up a disagreement (Rancière 1999, 124). When dissent persists after the deliberation process is over, it becomes essentialized into something that can only be dealt with through radical exclusion in order to maintain the illusion of consensus. Part of the problem for deliberative democrats is an unwillingness to acknowledge that all deliberations, no matter how inclusive, always must end in a decision which excludes other possibilities. Deliberative democrats try to dodge the responsibility of decision through claims that the end result can be a matter of consensus acceptable to all interested and rational parties (Mouffe 2009, 105). Politics will always have winners and losers, as no single outcome can ever please everyone due to the reality of plurality. Making claims that such decisions can be matters of broad consent will only push individuals away from the political process, as their dissent goes unacknowledged, which could push them towards violence. In the case of activist groups which utilize consensus-based decision making procedures, internal divisions will appear and the group dynamic can become toxic. Ironically, the embrace of conflict can enable better group cohesion as internal debates are considered healthy, not grounds for expulsion or self-censure.

The impracticality of arriving at a consensus decision is further complicated by issues of scale. The more people there are to be included in the deliberation, the harder it gets to reconcile divergent opinions, to the point where consensus-based decision making could not possibly extend beyond the scope of a handful of people. As numbers are scaled up, consensus-based decision making also begins to take more and more time, which can exclude those who wish to take part but simply have other things to do. When organizational meetings drag on due to the difficulty of reaching any kind of consensus, people with children or jobs can be inadvertently excluded, simply because they cannot dedicate all their free time to activism. So, while the internet can help overcome the issues of scale traditionally associated with participatory politics, it would actually be counterproductive for a consensus model, as more participants decrease the possibility of consensus. The only way to arrive at a consensus on any significant scale would be to deny human plurality and either posit everyone as essentially the same, or to paint all political issues as uncontroversial and having only one objectively correct answer which can be arrived at through computerized calculations.

Underestimating the significance of plurality as a source of disagreement undermines the idea that consensus is more inclusive to minority voices, as without a plurality of opinions there can be no minorities to begin with. If everyone is essentially the same, and disagreements will not arise stemming from differences in perspective and experience, then the idea of consensus in politics would not even be necessary. No politics would be needed as the sameness of everyone would mean that no decision would be controversial and, instead of decision making, there would simply be an enacting of the consensus view. Politics as a decision making layer would be unnecessary, as the bureaucracy could simply act directly on the consensual will of the people. The entire reason politics is necessary is because it provides a mechanism to make decisions on controversial issues on which people have differing positions. Eliminate the differing positions and the whole reason to have politics in the first place disappears.

Contrary to the inclusive intention of consensual thought, the persistence of conflict enables a wider array of voices and perspectives to be heard. As Barker argues, the ability to publicly present disagreement and engage in conflict enables the outsider to speak and forces the majority to consider its own status in relation to that of the outsider, thus expanding its sympathetic boundaries (Barker 2009, 38). Rather than the outsider being an ethical victim who is to be acted on by the majority so that they are no longer outside or disagreeable to the community, the outsider must be empowered to open up a conflict with the majority through the expression of dissent. In presenting this conflict with the social whole, the outsider is able to address the whole as an equal. The very ability to present a conflict in this manner is a demonstration of equality which can undermine any claims that the outsider's exclusion is legitimate.

5.3 Reconciliation and the Political Death Drive

Part of the drive behind the various anti-political theories which seek to eliminate conflict is a desire to arrive at a final reconciliation and simply be done with vexing political questions altogether. Politics and conflict are linked to risk, and the goal of these theories is to design institutions that create stability in order to allow people to engage in their private lives free from the entanglements of politics (Honig 1993, 2). As Honig goes on to argue, Rawls's political theory of reconciliation is appealing because it 'promises to satisfy a deep yearning, a yearning for peace and quiet, for the privacy of withdrawal so many liberals have sought throughout the history of liberal thinking' (Honig 1993, 198). What is missing in the liberal tradition is the idea that politics is empowering and satisfies the need to distinguish ourselves as unique subjects by freely engaging with others. If politics is assumed from the start to be a burden, then naturally doing away with it altogether would seem to be the ideal solution.

Along with the desire to be left alone to engage in private pursuits, the desire to reconcile conflict once and for all finds expression in the wish to do away with the uncertainty that stems from political conflict. Plurality is linked to natality, as each new person who comes into the world is unique and different, which spurs conflict and political uncertainty (Arendt 1998, 7–9). In order to eliminate uncertainty, and thus the risk that goes along with plural actors acting in concert, the reconciliatory projects of both Rawls and Habermas need to imagine a situation where plurality is done away with. Even when posited as a self-regulating ideal, reconciliatory political projects become a 'self-refuting ideal', as their realization would be their disintegration (Mouffe 2009, 32). To conceive of a politics of reconciliation, free of political conflict and uncertainty, is to conceive of a politics without politics. Political participation in a reconciliatory system is nonsensical: if there are no conflicts and nothing to debate because the institutions are so well designed, there is nothing political left to do. In order to ensure that politics remains dynamic and is a means to bring about change, the idea that there could be a time when society is so well ordered that dissent simply would not arise must be abandoned. Without conflict and dissent, there is nothing but stagnation.

Asserting the persistence of conflict can be troubling to some, as it can seem like politics is nothing but arguing without any advancement toward a goal. Since no final reconciliation of conflict can be possible because creating such a perfect society would require the elimination of plurality, the goal of political action should be to focus on individual issues. On this register, political conflict works in a similar manner to Freud's concept of the death drive. In Lacan's interpretation, we always circle around the cause of our desire without ever actually obtaining it, as to obtain it is to terminate the desire that drove us to pursue it in the first place (Lacan 1981). In political terms, an ultimate reconciliation of all conflict, expressed in the termination of the desire to act politically and open a dispute, is to give over to the death drive and thus die. While we will inevitably derive some pleasure and satisfaction from the conflicts we win (Lacan's jouissance), to try to achieve the satisfaction of eliminating all conflict negates the entire process, in the same way as a drug user overdosing and dying negates his or her ability to derive satisfaction from the temporary high of the drug. Political conflict must be approached in the same way Freud recommends navigating between the pleasure principle and the death drive. In *Civilization and its Discontents* he argues that 'the programme of becoming happy, which the pleasure principle imposes on us, cannot be fulfilled; yet we must not—indeed, we cannot—give up on our efforts to bring it nearer to fulfilment by some means or other' (Freud 1991, 271). This should be the method of political activists, always trying to bring about a better future, while recognizing that no final reconciliation or perfected society is possible.

The empowering aspect of politics that derives from revealing oneself as a unique subject by participating politically is contingent on the perpetual existence of an agonistic political sphere. The desire to appear publicly and have one's opinions heard is motivated by disagreement, and, as such, without the ability to express dissent and engage in political conflict the ability to participate and to reveal oneself as a unique political subject is lost. In a truly consensual system there is little motivation to actually participate, as adding yet another public 'yes!' to the overwhelming chorus of yesses makes no impact and does not reveal an individual as a unique subject but as a faceless member of the herd. It is precisely the ability to say something different and, thus initiate a conflict that provides political subjectivity and participation with their empowering characteristics. Far from being a necessary evil, conflict provides the outlet through which subjects distinguish themselves, thus empowering people to participate in the freedom of political action. To give up the ability to take part in this political process in the name of final reconciliations, is to allow politics to die.

5.4 Echo Chambers and Filter Bubbles

If conflict is not only necessary for politics, in that it provides the entire reason for its existence, as well as having a productive role in fostering plurality and subject formation, the next question, then, is how such an agonistic politics would play out in the online context that I have been arguing is necessary to revitalize a more robust form of politics. Two opposing arguments are generally presented to dismiss the suitability of online politics with respect to conflict. Both of these arguments confuse the software and hardware layers and, thus, extrapolate the experience of one group of users on a specific website to argue that the internet has a certain essence that makes it inherently incompatible with conflictual politics. The first branch of this argument argues that the ability to customize and personalize one's experience on the internet turns it into an echo chamber where people are able to isolate themselves from conflicting views and only visit sites and talk to people who already agree with them. The second argument, which will be dealt with in a later section, positions the internet as having too much conflict, thus making politics impossible. Both of these arguments are grounded in real experiences, and many people do use the internet in these manners, but as is demonstrated by the fact that these two arguments about the nature of the internet are in direct contradiction, the internet remains a space which can be produced in a number of ways, some of which are productive to politics, some of which are not.

One of the more prominent versions of the echo chamber argument was put forth by American legal scholar Cass Sunstein in his 2001 and 2009 books *Republic.com* and *Republic.com 2.0*. Sunstein argues that the personalization technology of the internet, from Google News to personalized book recommendations on Amazon.com, work to create a kind of insulated bubble around people, where everything is customized to their tastes and they end up not seeing anything that might challenge their point of view (Sunstein 2009, 3–6). Customization can act as an almost accidental tool that simply ends up reinforcing a user's already established beliefs, thereby undermining the pluralistic clash of opinions needed for a healthy democratic politics. Sunstein goes on to point to examples from terrorist groups and conspiracy theorists using websites as gathering places where their own views gain reinforcement from like-minded people. Sunstein's fear is that echo chambers will lead to a situation where 'diverse groups are seeing and hearing quite different points of view, or focusing on quite different topics, mutual understanding might be difficult, and it might be increasingly hard for people to solve problems that society faces together' (2009, 56). Echo chambers such as this have certainly become a problem, especially on social media, as people seek out others to reinforce their own beliefs and prejudices.

Echo chambers are not new of course, as broadcast media has always operated as an echo chamber which bounced around a very narrow band of possible political viewpoints. The internet has simply enabled there to be more echo chambers beyond the one that happens to align with the dominant beliefs of capital and the state. The issue of echo chambers became prominent in the aftermath of the 2016 American election, as many liberals blamed the election of Donald Trump on Facebook echo chambers which were circulating 'fake news' which was seen as deceiving people into voting for Trump. Echo chambers enable ideology to bounce around and reinforce itself, and thus the internet has enabled a break from the traditional structure where the broadcast media is able to control the ideological apparatus that is experienced by most of the population. Many liberals upset about the election of Trump were simply lamenting the fact that their preferred ideological echo chambers no longer held as much sway. The solution here is to enable spaces that accept and embrace conflicting views. People seek out alternative echo chambers when they feel their point of view is being ignored by the mainstream.

A major problem with the idea of echo chambers is the argument that people prefer them and thus will always actively seek them out rather than going to spaces of conflict. This is an argument made not only by Sunstein but various scholars doing work on online community, and states that people will predominantly seek out discussion groups online which reinforce their own opinions. Wojcieszak states that it is simply 'widely known' that people will seek discussion in order to reinforce their own views and then goes on to argue that the chatrooms and message boards are particularly problematic in this respect (Wojcieszak 2010, 638). While many such closed groups certainly proliferate across the internet, it is by no means a settled notion that people prefer discussion with like-minded people when it comes to politics. A brief look at Reddit, the largest such message board on the internet, demonstrates this point. The forum /r/politics, which is dedicated to American politics in general and which has frequent and often bitter conflicts of opinion across the political spectrum currently has around 3 million subscribers. By contrast, subforums dedicated to specific positions which would encompass those discussed on the more general American politics forum are much less popular. Democrats has a mere 11,000 subscribers, Liberal 19,000, Progressives 34,000, Conservative 35,000, Republican 14,000, and Libertarian 115,000. While the US election led to the creation of large subreddits dedicated to Donald Trump and Bernie Sanders, thus increasing polarization and creating echo chamber effects, the same period also saw the creation of a number of new subreddits dedicated to open discussion across the political spectrum. The numbers for Canadian-related political discussion are even more dramatic, as subreddits dedicated to individual parties and views have in the order of hundreds of subscribers, while the more general /r/canada has close to 150,000 subscribers and /r/CanadaPolitics has 14,000. If people were truly looking to avoid conflict and simply have their own views reinforced, then one would expect the ideologically homogenous subreddits to be much more popular than the general forums which contain frequent clashes of a variety of different opinions. Given the partisan nature of electoral politics, it is likely that echo chambers are more of a reflection of the party-driven structure than of the internet itself or of any basic human drives.

Even then, Sunstein's point about customization technology is not really new, as political dissenters have been publishing their own newspapers and pamphlets, trying to break people out of the mass media echo chamber for as long as mass media has existed. The more interesting problem of conflict happens within the internal dynamics of groups dedicated to a specific viewpoint or cause. In many cases chat rooms, social network groups, and discussion forums simply replicate existing group structures where there is some kind of explicit or implicit structure of authority. In an online context, people who join an activist group, for example, but who consistently go against the prevailing opinion may simply be banned or blocked from participating or even viewing the website, in the same manner people can get kicked out of political parties or blocked from attending organizational meetings. While the internet makes it easier to facilitate such groups, it also makes it easier to simply ban a person and never have to deal with him or her again, something that is problematic for advocates of agonistic politics. Political groups which favour internal consensus-based decision making models, such as Occupy Wall Street, would have a much easier time banning people from the movement's online spaces than it would from a physical protest.

Issues like these are more dangerous to the expression of diverse views and the existence of plurality because they can enable censorship, not because of accidental over-customization at the software level, but by actually putting too much authority into the hands of the human element. The best online political discussion forums are ones which are either moderated socially via their algorithmic design or ones in which human moderators have extremely limited authority and a very well-defined role. In systems where there must always be a present moderator, especially where politics is discussed, the temptation to censor disagreement is simply too high for most people to resist. Recent moderator scandals on Reddit demonstrate this problem. In 2014, the moderators of /r/politics were found to be deleting stories from sources they deemed to lack journalistic standards. Posting news or opinion pieces from sites such as Salon, Reason, and MotherJones were subject to automatic removal (Auerbach 2014). During this time, the moderators of /r/technology were found to be removing all stories related to Edward Snowden, the NSA spying scandal, and anything related to discussions on net neutrality (Alfonso 2014). In 2016 after the terrorist attack on an Orlando nightclub, the moderators of /r/news deleted almost every single comment and post about the shooting, raising the ire of Reddit's management team. Users of these forums revolted, and the top level Reddit administrators banned some of the moderators responsible for the censorship. The smaller the community, however, the less recourse there is to deal with abusive moderation. Reddit is caught in something of a contradiction as they still use human moderators, while at the same time their social ranking algorithm is meant to democratically moderate submissions to the site.

Discussion and debate forums where there are no human moderators or where their role is clearly defined are much more open to the expression of conflicting viewpoints because of the lack of censorship or appeals to the authority of the moderator to remove certain content. Instead, people have to confront uncomfortable and conflicting opinions head on, and attempt to persuade and debate rather than censor and banish. Investing authority in a small group of people to moderate discussion is anti-democratic, as there is usually little recourse against abuse. Many discussion sites, including many on Reddit, operate more as miniature kingdoms which enable moderators to exert their control over others. The problem of attempting to eliminate plurality from online forums is squarely an issue with how people are using and producing these spaces, and not an inherent flaw within the technology. Designing better discussion sites and promoting more egalitarian political structures online will solve many problems related to censorship as destructive of plurality.

A more nuanced version of the echo chamber effect is pointed to by Eli Pariser, who argues that the internet can cut people off from opposing views not because it enables people to join insular communities and customize away opposing views but because some of the biggest websites are automatically filtering away content we may not like behind the scenes (Pariser 2011). One of the best examples of such behind the scenes filtering is the order of search results on Google. The same search will show results in a different order depending on whether one is logged into one's Google account or not, and depending on which localization of Google one is using. Facebook is another target of Pariser's critique, as their timeline is filtered and ordered in such a way that may hide news stories that a conservative friend posts if one fills out the detailed profile and lists liberal as one's political viewpoint. While such filtering can be problematic, as Pariser explains, in the context of using the internet as a conflictual political realm there is no reason to replicate such a structure in a non-transparent manner on a political discussion site. While one may get fewer opposing views when looking at their social networks or searching for information, these are somewhat peripheral issues which demand algorithmic awareness, rather than arguments against the capacity to have a conflictual online political realm. If people rarely encounter opposing views outside of their political involvement, then this means that a conflictual online political realm is even more important, as it would be a place that would purposely expose people to contrasting opinions and different points of view. Social networking sites make for a poor political realm to begin with, and thus the problem of algorithmic filtering of opposing political viewpoints from our Facebook news feeds would again be solved by having an actual space of political conflict and thus not having to try to cram politics into a social structure where it simply does not fit.

Another version of the echo chamber argument is presented by Mouffe, who, although she acknowledges that the internet remains open and is not inherently consensual or conflictual, still maintains that most people simply use the internet to reinforce their own views and that the only way to truly confront opposing ideas and opinions is in person (Díaz Álvarez and Mouffe 2010). Of course, if people go looking for opinion reinforcement online, why would they not do the same offline? Other than that somewhat obvious contradiction, it is precisely the ability to enhance the number of opportunities to encounter difference that works as one of the internet's main agonistic strengths. Contrary to Mouffe's claim that we find more conflicting views in offline space, the internet actually provides ease of entry into a proliferation of different worlds and can create spaces of actual political debate which contain a plurality of different viewpoints. If someone wants to debate some particular issue and see what other people think about it, where do they go in offline space to do so? There are no designated and widely accessible spaces for political discussion where a plurality of people can be found. Official sites of politics are restricted in access, universities are not accessible to the average person wanting to discuss the issue of the day, and it is unreasonable to expect random people in public spaces to be willing to discuss politics. By contrast, there are widely recognized spaces on the internet which are devoted to political discussion that one can enter at will and find others willing to discuss these issues. As a wide-scale and sustained political realm where agonistic pluralism is actually practical, the possibilities outside of the internet are extremely limited in scope, to the point that they could never serve as a political alternative to the status quo.

In addition to the availability of conflictual spaces online, the face to face element that Mouffe advocates actually hinders disagreement because in person communication is often biased by the desire to get along. It is much easier to disagree with an anonymous argument online than it is to disagree and debate political issues with your friends or coworkers. Often people take disagreement personally, and a clash of opinions can alienate friends and acquaintances, thus hurting one's social position. Political speech and action are risky and require courage. The shield of anonymity has been, and continues to be, essential to the expression of dissenting points of view. If politics is to maintain its agonistic edge and not devolve into anti-political consensus, then making it easier to take part by shielding one's private life from one's public statements is necessary. If one cannot make dissenting statements without social ramifications, then the freedom to participate and reveal oneself as a unique subject will be lost in a sea of conformity dictated by the tyranny of the social majority.

5.5 Passion and Rationality

The basis for the idea of consensus within the deliberative democratic framework comes from the assumption of rationality. In a Habermasian 'ideal speech situation,' consensus outcomes that can be generally accepted by all interested parties are guaranteed by both the ability to engage in uncoerced speech and the assumed rationality of those deliberating (Habermas 1985, 25–26). While Habermas certainly recognizes that such ideal situations may not always be realizable, calling the ideal speech situation a 'regulative ideal,' the general practicality of rational consensus must still be questioned (Habermas 1994b, 51). By treating political issues as rationally solvable and subject to consensus, deliberation becomes more about unmasking ideologies so that people can set aside what is blinding them from the objective answer. However, even if it were possible to get everyone in a deliberation to be rational, why would rational individuals necessary agree on any political decision? Agonistic pluralism recognizes that people who share a common world will still engage in conflicts in which there is no rational resolution. Deliberative democracy positions itself against the antagonistic extreme which argues that those who disagree have no common world and thus there can be no grounds for deliberation, but what is left out is the middle position of agonism which accepts that plurality means that there will always be disagreement (Mouffe 2005, 20).

By positing deliberation in terms of ideals, either in the Habermasian sense described above, or in Rawls's formulation of the original position, there is a sense that by making people equal, they become the same. With Rawls especially, conflict is seen as stemming from major institutional injustices such as economic or social inequality. Through imagining ourselves in an 'original position' behind a 'veil of ignorance', Rawls argues we can rationally come to a set of consensus institutions (Rawls 1999, 37–46). The assumption is that differences in political opinion stem from institutional inequality, and that once those differences are stripped away, people are all basically the same. Rational disagreement, which is accepted as a fact stemming from plurality in the agonistic approach, is assumed away. Not only does the assumption of rationality and equality leading to consensus eliminate the potential for real political conflict, but it also assumes away a large part of politics. The Rancièrian politics of fighting to be recognized as politically capable in the first place is set aside. If anti-politics operates through policing the boundaries to ensure that those who are deemed unqualified to speak remain in their place, politics in Rancière's formulation involves fighting for the ability to speak politically. Before there can be a deliberation on any political issue, there is 'the dispute over the existence of the dispute and the parties confronting each other in it' (Rancière 1999, 55). When the nature of the dispute itself is not considered to be a political dispute itself, as when Habermas and Rawls posit ideal situations of rationality, then the danger is that those who persist in the metadispute are cast out as irrational or morally backwards (Mouffe 2005, 84–85).

Even though increasing public participation is meant to be a strength of deliberative democracy, Habermas argues that it is the rationally acceptable results of deliberation, rather than its mechanisms for participation, which are the source of its legitimacy (Habermas 2001, 121). If outcomes of political disputes can be a matter of rational consensus, then why is participation in the deliberation process even needed? If it is assumed that legitimacy stems from rationality and that political problems can be solved in a way agreeable to all involved, then minimizing the empirical obstacles to ideal rationality would increase legitimacy. Human participation in deliberative democracy becomes its greatest flaw. To achieve a more legitimate form of deliberative democracy, an algorithm could be designed which would take a broad range of complex inputs representing the interests and situations of all people involved in any political dispute, and then produce a rationally acceptable consensus solution to the problem. Such an algorithm, programmed on a sufficiently powerful computer, would eliminate the empirical obstacles of human bias and practical irrationality that impede the ideal speech situation. If rationally consensual positions are possible, then using a computer program would streamline and speed up the rather inefficient deliberation process. So long as the algorithm is designed in such a way, perhaps using Rawls's original position and veil of ignorance devices, that it is a matter of rational consensus, its results would be more legitimate than humans deliberating. In an ideal sense, deliberative democracy would replace all human participation, and in fact politics as a whole, with sufficiently advanced computer programs. Such an outcome is in stark contrast to the agonistic approach advanced here, which seeks to use computers to enhance human participation rather than eliminate it altogether.

In contrast to the deliberative approach, legitimacy in the version of politics that I am advocating stems from both the lack of barriers to participate politically and the acceptance of conflict. In deliberative democracy, irreconcilable conflicts of opinion on decisions are positioned as a threat to the legitimacy of the system, as, if all do not agree, then consensus is impossible and the system is called into question. Given that eliminating such conflicts is practically impossible, the real question to ask is what level of conflict is politically legitimate? Agonistic pluralism generates legitimacy by providing an arena in which individuals can disagree, and thus the ability to engage in political conflict is what provides the political realm with its legitimacy (Mouffe 2005, 20). Conflict only becomes illegitimate if it spills outside of the realm of debate and persuasion and into the realm of coercive force. Such antagonistic conflict is illegitimate because it threatens the existence of politics itself. By failing to differentiate agonistic and antagonistic forms of conflict, deliberative democracy's stance against conflict is anti-political.

The demand for rationality in politics, represented by this robotic ideal of eliminating humans from the decision making process altogether, is related to the desire to purge passions from politics. It may be beneficial that computer programs could replace humans in a deliberative democratic system because in a politics that demands rigid rationality there would be little motivation for people to participate. An emphasis on consensus and rationality, as in deliberative democracy, prevents the passionate attachment to a cause that spurs so much political participation (Mouffe 2009, 103–104). People are motivated to get involved in politics not through the prospect of setting aside individual opinions and attempting to arrive at a rational consensus, but through taking a side in a dispute and arguing that one's own opinion is correct. By producing 'conflictual representations of the world,' an agonistic politics can mobilize people to participate by channeling their passions into agonistic political causes, rather than antagonistic conflicts over identity, religion, or culture (Mouffe 2005, 25).

While the deliberative democrats seek to strip politics of its passion in the name of rationality, the advocates of treating politics ironically wish to purge passion in the name of making politics safer. The common reference point for many of these thinkers, Lyotard and Rorty especially, is the Holocaust. All passionate political commitments are viewed through the lens of the past and proto-totalitarian impulses are discovered everywhere. Thus, Rorty constantly reminds us not to take our opinions too seriously because passionate attachment to a cause is what led to the Nazis and the Holocaust (Barker 2009, 100–101). Lyotard similarly recasts the promise of future emancipation as a past lie that resulted in 'infinite crime' whose only response is a process of 'endless mourning' (cited in Rancière 2009a, 130). Purging political passion in the name of preventing totalitarian catastrophe also purges passionate commitment to progressive causes that can make the world a better place. The result of these demands to look back, is an inability to move forward. Only by embracing agonistic conflict is progress possible.

5.6 Flame Wars and Civility

Stemming from the idea that politics involves passionate attachments is the flip side of the echo chamber argument, which positions the internet as too rife with conflict. This argument states that political discussion will get washed away in the anonymous and unaccountable 'flame wars' that will inevitably erupt every time anyone disagrees online. This line of reasoning argues that because the shield of anonymity enables courage, people are not afraid to act uncivilized and, thus, instead of political debate, conflict turns into the trading of personal insults. This view is advanced by Richard Davis, who argues that the nature of online discussion promotes 'vigorous attack and humiliation' and, as such, leads to most discussion turning into belligerent flaming which turns people off who want to actually discuss ideas and political issues (Davis 1999, 163). Davis goes on to argue that the prominence of flaming or insults in place of actual discussion is driven by anonymity and its associated lack of accountability, making it a problem with the internet in general. The internet is positioned as a kind of Hobbesian state of nature where the lack of authority stemming from the allegedly unaccountable nature of online anonymity leads to a nasty and brutish existence which is wholly unsuitable to civilized political disagreement. While I have dealt with the argument against anonymity previously and found it to have little theoretical weight, recent studies have shown that knowing the identity of the other person has little impact on the potential for flaming, as having one's views directly challenged was cited as the primary factor leading to flaming (Hutchens, Cicchirillo, and Hmielowski 2014, 9). While attempts to simply link anonymity to incivility fail to explain much, the issue of political disagreement becoming uncivilized and leading to flame wars is a common occurrence online which deserves further attention. Transforming antagonism into political agonism is the goal of agonistic pluralism, thus the creation of antagonism out of political agonism online is an interesting case to consider.

Some advocates of deliberative democracy, with its goal of developing rational consensus, have similarly argued that online discussion is simply too conflictual or 'nasty' and that democratic politics is hindered when it is placed online (Anderson et al. 2014). Such arguments frame democratic deliberation as a sterile and unemotional affair, which is not only an unrealistic ideal but also an undesirable one. By contrast, the conflictual status of politics naturally stirs people's emotions, as people become passionately attached to causes and sides in a conflict. Sometimes these passions may overflow, leading to conflict that turns personal and harms political debate. While such breakdowns in politeness as a result of passion are not helpful, they are also not the catastrophe they are made out to be by deliberative critics of the internet or those seeking to paint the internet as a site of moral panic. The fact that people who are passionate about an issue may get frustrated and throw out some insults in the course of a political discussion is not the end of the world, and, at least in an online context, can be ignored by the rest of the participants in favour of focusing on more substantial conversations. While such disruptions can be off-putting or annoying, they are not capable of imposing a certain viewpoint through force, and can be contained without threatening the political process itself.

Too much emphasis is placed on these passionate overflows by many critics interested in claiming that online politics is impossible (Smith 2011). The spectre of the dreaded flame war is raised, in which all pretense to political discussion is dropped and the involved parties end up drowning out those trying to engage in actual issues by posting a constant stream of insults. Is this, however, an accurate characterization of online debate which condemns the entire medium as politically unsuitable? While there is certainly a fair bit of insult trading in online political debates, it is actually not that disruptive and the majority are able to engage in conflictual yet civil disagreements.

In Papacharissi's analysis of political themed Usenet discussion groups, she found that while these discussions had a tendency to become impolite as arguments got heated (swearing, insults, sarcasm, etc.), they tended to remain civil

(Papacharissi 2004). Civility was defined as not threatening other individuals, respecting their basic rights, and not making comments which would be deemed offensive to social groups, such as racist or sexist comments (Papacharissi 2004, 267). As she goes on to argue, the examples of uncivil comments and behaviour which were impeccably polite were much more disturbing. She pointed to one discussion in particular, where discussants were calm and polite to each other but were promoting white supremacy and arguing that large groups of people should be denied their basic human rights (Papacharissi 2004, 279). In this sense, as long as heated discussions do not become threatening to the participants or devolve into petty bigotry, but instead remain isolated to impoliteness toward another discussant they can be tolerated and ignored by the majority without threatening the civility of political debate altogether. Sites which offer more user interaction, such as Reddit, tend to be more civil than sites without user interaction, such as newspaper comments sections. When one can post uncivil comments in a manner which goes unchallenged, there is a likelihood that behaviour will continue, whereas getting challenged in the form of direct replies or other social punishments, as in Reddit downvotes, can influence users to avoid such behaviour, in order to maintain a positive reputation. Unaccountability stems not from anonymity, but from a lack of interactivity which allows uncivil comments to go unchallenged.

The focus of debates on the suitability of online political conflict should be on whether or not they are civil rather than simply polite. Civility is accepting of conflict and passionate disagreement but seeks to limit the extremes of threats and attacks on basic rights in order to create a public space where people can be free to speak their mind without their identity or person coming under discriminatory attack (Balibar 2011, 30). Following Balibar on this point, we need not view the plurality of conflictual subjects as intrinsically prone to violence or incivility that must be tamed with a strong top-down government in the manner of Hobbes. Political civility, by contrast, can be democratic and bottom up in that it is derived from 'joining' the political realm, rather than having membership in it (Balibar 2011, 31). By actively joining the political realm, as opposed to simply being born into it, there is a sense that one is partly responsible for its upkeep and existence, which can generate a bottom-up form of civility, which as Balibar explains, has driven the state to become more civil and less cruel (Balibar 2011, 33).

The demand for politeness in political debate often amounts to a demand not to disagree, for in polite company one does not raise controversial political issues. Thus politics need not be polite, it only needs to be civil, because an obsession with politeness can lead to censorship and constrained expression. Again this idea of civility and politeness speaks to how such a political forum is organized and moderated. When the role of moderators is enforcing politeness, there can be serious consequences for people who are passionately presenting an argument. Such passionate debates can quickly become censored, as the 'tone' of the participants may be deemed impolite and lead to removal.

Bringing up certain controversial ideas may also be deemed as impolite because the majority or moderators may not want to discuss them. Going to a forum dedicated to a specific viewpoint and presenting critiques of that viewpoint is often deemed impolite, resulting in censorship in the name of maintaining the established consensus.

Since passionate conflicts of opinion are interesting and mobilize people to get politically involved, they should be encouraged. The internet's proclivity as a medium to produce more avenues for conflict makes it well suited for an agonistic conception of politics. The advocates of politeness often seem willing to tolerate incivility, which is truly destructive to political discourse, in the name of politeness. Those who argue that online political debate is too impolite and that the internet is unsuitable to politics are not any different from those who argue that protests which have confrontations with the police are impolite and thus are not suitable avenues for politics. The argument from politeness is part of a wider anti-political argument against any form of political conflict, and its application to the internet is simply its most recent manifestation. If we accept a little bit of impoliteness now and then as the cost of ensuring passionate mobilization, then the primary concern is whether online debate remains civil, which for the most part, can be accomplished if effort is put toward that goal. There is, however, a rather notorious complication for online political conflict that can disrupt and derail entire forums and debates: the figure of the troll.

5.7 Trolls, Gadflies, and Political Conflict

A seemingly unique aspect of online political discussion is the phenomenon of the troll. The troll is a complicated figure but is generally viewed as someone who enters a discussion for the sole purpose of disrupting it. Politically speaking, trolling occupies a liminal position, as the expression of legitimate dissent is often considered disruptive and gets labelled as trolling, which can muddle the entire idea of what trolling is and whether it actually is harmful to political debate or not. What exactly trolling consists of is a contested notion and various definitions exist, which vary based on context. Donath defines trolling as related to identity deception and uses examples from social forums where an individual takes on a false persona in order to upset the other users (Donath 1999, 42). While adopting an insincere identity is certainly an aspect of trolling, within a political context, trolls tend to be more flexible. Donath's definition is problematic for the case of a political troll who maintains a consistent username and presence, but will say anything necessary to annoy others. For the political troll, being flexible is more important than creating a false identity. A troll interested in disrupting a political discussion and provoking emotional responses does not need to maintain a consistent false identity, or even any identity at all, as the troll will argue whatever position that he or she feels will annoy the target of the trolling the most. The same troll will take radical left-wing positions when arguing with a conservative, and then take radical right-wing positions when arguing with a leftist.

Bergstrom further complicates the idea of trolling as identity deception in her report on a Reddit user who was ostracized for trolling, but claimed his trolling was not meant to deceive people but was a work of interactive fiction (Bergstrom 2011). In the situation described by Bergstrom, the user saw himself as playing a character, while allowing others to believe that this character was actually his real identity. Identity deception which is not meant to be disruptive would be less of a problem on politically-oriented discussion sites, as the user's real identity is less important than the arguments being presented. While it may be strange, and even unlikely, to adopt a character and consistently play it within a political context, there is no reason to believe that such deception would be disruptive. A big part of trolling, as Coleman points out, is creating a spectacle (Coleman 2012). Such spectacles tend to be disruptive of political discussion, but a single person playing a consistent character that no one knows is a fake identity is less likely to become a spectacle in a political context as compared to a social setting. Combining some aspects of the deception and spectacle definitions, I define a political troll as someone who enters an online political forum with the sole intent of provoking emotional responses from people by saying whatever is necessary to generate a reaction, resulting in actual political discussion becoming sidetracked. A troll is essentially someone who seeks to transform political agonism back into social antagonism, therefore threatening the sustainability of political discourse.

A troll, by definition, is not a conflictual political actor because the troll does not seek to reveal him or herself as a unique political subject motivated by the desire to share his or her opinions with others. In this sense, provocation is not necessarily trolling, as the intent may be political, while for a troll the intent is personal amusement. When a leftist visits a discussion forum predominantly inhabited by conservatives for the sole purpose of picking arguments, that leftist is not a troll because the intent to provoke is derived from the wish to engage in political debate as a result of sincerely held opinions. Dahlberg's definition of trolls as disruptive infiltrators is also too broad, as in this example the leftist would be disrupting the consensual proceedings of the conservative forum and thus be labelled as a troll (Dahlberg 2001b). From a deliberative point of view, persistent disruptions and dissent with the purpose of blocking the achievement of rational consensus can get labelled trolling, even if such disruptions are the expression of sincerely held beliefs. From an agonistic point of view, such expressions of dissent would be considered legitimate political expression and not trolling.

A troll cannot simply be a political opponent or a person who is generally impolite in the context of a political debate. Someone who might be quick to anger and has a tendency to become impolite is not a troll, so long as the impoliteness and anger stem from sincerely held beliefs and the person is not trying to shut down the conversation altogether. The annoyance people feel when they realize they have been tricked into engaging in a discussion with someone who legitimately does not care and was simply trying to provoke a reaction feeds the negative attitude toward trolling and can lead to muddled definitions, where a troll becomes anyone who positions themselves against the majority. In this sense, to accuse someone of trolling and insincerity can become an anti-political method of shutting down legitimate debate itself. Labelling an opponent a troll and then appealing to others to not engage with or to not 'feed the troll' can play on negative associations with trolling to effectively expel someone from a discussion in an unwarranted manner (Bergstrom 2011). Calling someone a troll, with the purpose of preventing that person from participating in a debate is disruptive, and can be a form of trolling itself.

While engaging in pointless arguments with someone who is simply trying to provoke you for personal amusement can be extremely frustrating and devalue the seriousness of political debate, the almost universal condemnation of trolling needs to be more closely examined in the context of political conflict. In this sense, we can ask if trolling has any redeeming value, and the answer may not obviously be no. In some cases, the troll is willing to put forward controversial views that, even if not actually supported by the troll, can give participants practice in arguing against extreme positions which rarely get expressed. The troll can also force subjects to examine their own viewpoints and help them find problems in their own opinions. It may be more useful to consider trolling not in absolute terms, but on a gradient from disruptively anti-political to relatively mild expressions of insincerity.

Holmes attempts to link such milder forms of online trolling to Rancière's concept of dissensus, but does so through an analysis of a group whose position is thoroughly ironipolitical, in that their goal is essentially to keep the internet from becoming a site of serious political practice (Holmes 2013). What Holmes takes as a repartitioning of the online sensible is actually the attempt to enforce, through trolling, the prevailing anti-political norm of online space as a playground and, thus, as entirely non-political. According to Holmes's interpretation, the offline equivalent to what he thinks an online troll is doing would be the police breaking up a protest and setting things back to normal. The dispersion of a serious protest is not a redistribution of the sensible but its end, as the temporary political disruption of a space is returned to its normal function. To interpret trolling in terms of Rancière's notion of politics as a distribution of the sensible, one might imagine a troll, who in the course of attempting to disrupt a political forum for his or her own amusement, ends up accidentally enhancing the level of discourse and seriousness of debate among the other participants. In the same way a work of art need not be explicitly political to have political consequences, a troll may lead people to sharpen their arguments and rethink their own positions, leading them to take politics more seriously as a way of frustrating trolling attempts.

According to the definition of trolling advanced here, Socrates seems to have been the original troll. While advancing no position or opinion of his own, Socrates went around Athens provoking the citizens by demonstrating that those who thought they were wise were actually not (Plato 1998, 21). The people of Athens clearly considered Socrates a troll. They denounced him for not putting forward any of his own opinions and only criticizing those of others. They claimed he was simply interested in causing a disturbance, and it could be argued that his supposed quest from the Delphic Oracle was simply Socrates's attempt to justify the pleasure he derived from annoying the Athenian elite. Socrates, however, saw his role as a gadfly whose annoying bites woke up the sluggish beast of Athenian public opinion, and for this Socrates claims he is doing a public service (Plato 1998, 31). Arendt argues that Socrates's *Apology* is one of the great examples of persuasive political speech in that Socrates saw a public role for the philosopher that differentiated him from Plato's hostility to politics (Arendt 2007, 7). Taken in this light, Socrates was less a troll than public critic who did not claim to have all the answers but, by asking questions, improved the level of political discourse in the *polis*. Socrates, if he was a troll, was a politically productive one as he sought to improve the opinions of the citizens for their own benefit, making this form of trolling rather mild and certainly not disruptive to the sustainability of political debate.

Even a gadfly which bites for its own benefit can have positive results, as such, the reaction to trolling must be contingent upon whether it has political or anti-political outcomes. If trolling turns into bullying or gets so disruptive that, rather than improving the opinions of people by forcing them to deal with uncomfortable questions, it makes people unwilling or unable to feel they can comfortably express their views, then it takes on an anti-political character and should not be tolerated. Milder Socratic-type trolling, however, may be allowed to persist so long as it stays mild. The methods of dealing with trolls are controversial, as, if left to moderators, personal bias can cloud who exactly is a troll or not, and, if left to public vote then the potential for more trial of Socrates situations is rife.[12] In many cases the best response is one of collective action against the pleasure the troll derives from their comments. This can work by ignoring known trolls, attempting to counter-provoke a troll, or simply responding to a suspected troll calmly and rationally by keeping one's emotions in check.

While trolling can be extremely disruptive, especially when it takes on an uncivil tone, in many ways mild forms of trolling can work as a political maturation process for adolescents and even movements as a whole. The young person who comes to an online discussion forum, not really having formed many opinions but curious about these public exchanges, may engage in trolling for their personal amusement, only to be drawn into actual debates by accident which can facilitate the opinion formation process and get that individual interested and involved in politics. Adolescent trolling can also operate as a kind of testing of opinions and used for practice making arguments, where the troll can try putting on a variety of different political hats in the course of trying to annoy people, only to find that one of those hats might fit quite well, leading the troll to abandon annoying people and actually start advocating for a cause and attempting to persuade others of his or her own opinions. In many ways, this trolling as maturation process was fully evidenced by the transformation of Anonymous from a form of organized collective trolling motivated by the desire to have some fun at other people's expense to a full on mature political movement (Coleman 2011). The participants in Anonymous came to realize that their actions can have consequences and that, if they wanted to maintain the internet as a space of freedom where one could have fun, they needed to treat it as a real space and fight for it politically.

Since conflict is essential for politics, as without disagreement and dissent politics would simply wither away into technocratic administration with no need for public debate or decision-making, the key question for an online politics is whether or not online political spaces can help foster productive forms of conflict. The answer is complicated, as different websites can produce different interactions which depend on how people want to use these spaces. Different algorithmic structures can also push people's behaviour in certain directions, with some algorithms facilitating hostility and others promoting civility. The internet has the potential to help foster more contentious political debate and disagreement, as it is able to connect more people from a plurality of viewpoints and make it easier to disagree and dissent through the shield of anonymity. The argument made by those critical of online politics that the internet is simply a forum for anonymous bullies and trolls to engage in personal attacks fails to recognize the real nature of conflict. People are more likely to say uncivil and hateful things when they cannot be challenged or contested, meaning that political discussion sites tend to have a much higher level of discourse than general one-way commenting sections such as on newspaper websites. The ability to challenge and disagree is essential for civil political discourse, as the ability to critique and debate those who make harmful comments can have a civilizing effect which can keep the topic focused on political matters. The internet as a medium can produce more impolite and heated exchanges, due to the potential duration of such encounters, but this is a small price to pay for having a space to actually disagree and debate political matters in the first place. New algorithmic structures designed specifically to manage online political discussion must be created to deal with trolling and incivility while also maintaining the ability to disagree. Too often online spaces fail to walk the middle ground between consensus-based censorship and toxic incivility.

CHAPTER 6

Steps toward the Digitization of Politics

Using the internet for political purposes, whatever they may be, is no longer a new phenomenon. As we have seen, the internet was indispensable for the Arab Spring protests, while the Occupy movement was able to harness the internet not just to get its message out, but to globalize itself and enable its themes to become part of the popular conversation. Meanwhile, Anonymous grew into a full-fledged political movement, with the internet as their primary site of engagement. Post-fascist movements have also taken shape online, with some directly incorporating certain elements of online trolling culture and aesthetics into their movement. The internet is also increasingly becoming a site of political dispute itself, as issues of net neutrality, privacy, and government spying are increasingly the topics of both government and public concern. While these are interesting developments in their own right, my main concern throughout has been with how politics might be reinvigorated and transformed into something more participatory and agonistic by placing it online. The goal was to outline a form of internet-enabled politics that would inspire engagement and empowerment, rather than cynicism and alienation.

By placing the common stage of politics online, old boundaries are erased and new possibilities emerge. Representation as the default position of realistic democracy no longer makes sense, as the asynchronous communication that is enabled by the internet allows both many more to take part and to do so at times and durations of their choosing. By having a common space on the internet accessible to all, people can have a place in which the exchange of political opinions can reveal who they truly are. With the opportunity to participate in debates and decisions on political matters, there is an opportunity for people to exercise the freedom to be political, rather than to be merely managed as bodies in a population. The common stage of online politics is one of conflict, where the passionate disagreement between adversaries can be expressed. Each

---

How to cite this book chapter:
Smith, T. G. 2017. *Politicizing Digital Space: Theory, The Internet, and Renewing Democracy.* Pp. 123–129. London: University of Westminster Press. DOI: https://doi.org/10.16997/book5.f. License: CC-BY-NC-ND 4.0

of these terrains, both in their online and offline expressions, can be configured in ways which make them more or less political. By focusing on these terrains of contestation, I have sought to ground my understanding of politics in these concrete practices in order to ensure that the reader is not left wondering what exactly politics involves. Doing so was also meant to clear up confusion over uses of the word politics which describe configurations of a terrain which are thoroughly anti-political.

Today, most of the popular websites that are analyzed for political potential tend to be social in nature. As I argued in the second chapter, the social realm is characterized by an inverted flowing together of public and private. We use Facebook to publicly reveal our most private information and thoughts. The social is the dominant configuration of offline space as well. Especially in North America, our 'public' spaces are increasingly spaces of shopping and commerce, which leave little room for expressions of politics. Given the difficulty of establishing new political spaces offline, to push the terrain of space toward more politicization we should focus our attention toward the internet. Why merely occupy existing space when we can create it altogether? While attempts to push offline space toward more political configurations are obviously extremely important, when thinking of establishing a more durable political configuration of this terrain the ability to create new spaces online is full of potential.

All of the four terrains of course tie into each other, and politicizations and depoliticizations in one terrain can spill into the others. By creating spaces of political engagement online, we can establish new forms of political subjectivity that are less available in an offline setting. The rise of post-fascism and the liberal concern with identity politics are both anti-political configurations of the terrain of subjectivity. Identity is what makes us the same as everyone else, whereas politics is about expressing our uniqueness. Given that identity so often lead to discrimination, more politicization must be pushed by promoting a form of universal empty subjectivity that disrupts both the attempt to discriminate negatively and positively based on identity. My argument in chapter three was that when we engage in political space online, we are often accidently pushed into a situation of universal emptiness in which our identity traits are unknown to others. To paraphrase Martin Luther King Jr., pseudonymous online political engagement has a way of forcing others to judge you by the content of your character rather than the colour of your skin, simply because the latter is unknown. Subjectivity can be politicized if we make a conscious effort to move toward a subjectivity based on the equality of emptiness.

Populist movements around the world are increasingly expressing the complications of the terrain of participation. On the one hand, these movements demonstrate that the old elite-driven neoliberal consensus of representative democracy has lost its credibility as people demand governments that are representative of regular people. On the other hand, these movements often manifest themselves in ways that lead to uninformed decisions, leading critics to caution that participation must be strictly limited. Such arguments are expressed in online forums as well, where often heavy handed moderators quash real participation while at the same time those who do participate often post uninformed or hateful comments. Thus, the terrain of participation is complicated when it comes to placing politics online, as we must be careful about what we mean by participation. In the fourth chapter I emphasized the fact that to politicize participation, it must be a combination of debate and decision. Simply enabling people to make decisions without forging an opinion through debate leads to uninformed gut reactions. At the same time, if people do take the time to engage with each other in a serious manner and thus develop informed decisions, they should be empowered to make decisions. While the other terrains often face opposition to politicization directly, most people want more participation. The key way to politicize this terrain is less about convincing people that participation in politics is positive, but about attempting to make this participation politically substantive. An online political realm could enable a participatory democracy in the sense of Arendt or Macpherson, but we are also seeing an influx of online participation that is resulting in depoliticizations.

How we participate online is largely shaped by how we approach the issue of conflict. When participating means that conflict is something to avoid, we end up with echo chambers which configure the terrain of conflict in less political ways. When participation leads to people who are a little too eager for conflict, the result can be trolling and harassment which reconfigures agonistic politics into antagonistic forms of abuse. If the terrain of conflict is a sliding scale, the needle must be kept in the middle for politics to flourish. The internet can open up conflictual spaces that simply cannot exist offline, where we can go to debate the issues of the day with people from around the world with various viewpoints. At the same time, the internet can also facilitate too little or too much conflict, and thus like the terrain of participation, conflict is an issue that has special complications when it is placed in an online context.

Taken together, these four terrains of contestation allow an elaboration of a theory of politics rooted in concrete elements that are not merely a manifestation of other realms of human activity. Politics happens in a dedicated political space open to subjects with no qualification who participate in conflictual speech through debate and take action through making decisions. By building such a theory of politics from the ground up by focusing on these terrains, I attempted to paint politics not as some abstract overall goal, but as bound up in the configuration of various elements of society. Reinvigorating politics is not some all or nothing proposition, but a matter of attempting to push toward more political configurations on a smaller scale in the hope that these politicizations can eventually build up into a situation that is overall more political than the status quo of representative democracy.

As has been my argument throughout, the internet as a technology provides an opportunity for change which must be shaped by human activity. The internet will not automatically reinvigorate politics, nor is it is entirely unsuited for political matters. Activists need to create political space online, as well as to defend and expand the openness of existing nascent spaces. While new online political realms will no doubt come about organically and take on unanticipated forms, there are existing spaces which I have used as examples of how some of the functions of such a political space could operate. In the academic scholarship, there is currently too much focus on social networking, given both its relative novelty and its heavy use by recent activist movements. The social nature of social networking makes it unsuitable to serve as anything but a communications tool, and future scholarship on online politics must look deeper. Pseudonymous discussion forums are where the true potential lies, and I have continually pointed to Reddit for practical examples of how online political discussion could operate.

The front page of Reddit collects and displays the most popular submissions from all the subforums the user has subscribed to. An online political structure could work in the same manner, with each regional level having its own forums, and allowing for the creation of forums dedicated to specific issues. In this sense, if someone was only interested in issues related to climate change as well as what was happening within their city and neighbourhood, they could subscribe to these three forums and not have to wade through discussions related to other issues or other regional levels which they were not interested in. At the same time, if this person saw that there was a major proposal related to climate change being discussed at a regional level different from what they were usually interested in, they could easily access that regional forum via the climate change forum to discuss the issue they were interested in without needing to be subscribed to it.

Each regional level, which could go from the neighbourhood level all the way up to the global scale, could have multiple forums with different purposes. There could be a general discussion forum through which people could raise issues for discussion which might warrant further debate and action. Such a forum would be more about responding to and discussing current events. A second level of forum would take issues which gained the most attention in the general discussion forum and invite proposals for action which could be debated and selected for a voting decision. To move from the first level to the second level forum, there could be a meta-vote attached to the issue in the general discussion forum which would allow certain issues to be nominated for more debate/decision if they reached a certain vote threshold. In the second level forum, the most prominent proposals and opinions would be re-presented for the purpose of being shaped into choices to vote on, and after a set period of time a set of options based on the discussion would be chosen. Developing the debate into options to vote on could be performed either by elected moderators or could be chosen based on the comments marked as potential proposals which received the highest proportion of agree to disagree votes. Winning proposals could then be moved to a third implementation forum, where the specifics of winning proposals could be discussed. This section might deal with issues of cost, budgeting, and specific policy implementation and be directed by civil servants with a speciality in the area, ensuring that proposals were properly costed, realistic, and within the operating budget.

A layered structure would also provide many options in terms of how much influence human moderators would have. Algorithms could be written in order to choose which issues were advanced to the debate/decision forum and how to choose which options would be available in votes. Alternatively, elected moderators could perform these tasks as well as bring forth cyclical issues, such as budgets, which would need to be periodically brought into the decision forum whether the issue was popular or not. While an algorithmic approach could eliminate the problems of moderator bias, having human moderators elevating issues could also ensure that important but less popular issues were acted on. The matter of dealing with trolls and comments that become uncivil is more difficult, as detecting such behaviours with algorithms is extremely difficult. At the same time, such behaviour often walks a fine line and is prone to interpretation. The goal should be to generate a bottom-up form of civility by empowering participants and giving them a real stake in what happens so as to make them feel responsible for keeping discussions civil. By contrast, people feel little responsibility for the quality of discussion on a website on which they feel like an intruder or on which they have little stake in its continued existence. Above all, civility must be a personal responsibility, however, for those who lack such feelings of responsibility, mechanisms can be created to flag and alert people of uncivil behaviour. In addition to the ability to agree or disagree with a button press, the ability to simply click an uncivil button to make the commenter aware that others feel they are overstepping the bounds of civility could be used as well, with persistent reports being escalated to moderator action. Matters such as these would have to be a matter of trial and error experimentation and some combination of the two approaches would likely work best. The structure of current systems of governance are generally too rigid for fear that the elected authorities will overstep their reach, but an online politics which replaces the authority of individuals with the power of groups could be more open to experimentation and tweaking of the structure to make it more effective. By adopting an iterative approach borrowed from software design, the constitutional framework could become innovative and adaptive, rather than rigid and constraining as it currently is.

With a multi-layered approach, people could easily choose to what degree they wished to participate without getting bogged down in aspects of the political process in which they lacked interest. Such a structure demonstrates the strengths of the understanding of politics which I have advocated in the previous chapters. By having a single online space which is recognized as political and with real decision making power, the biggest exclusionary obstacle to political engagement would be overcome. People would go to this space to test their opinions in debate and reveal themselves to be unique individuals by sharing their perspective on the common world with others. The various layers would provide multiple avenues and degrees of participation, allowing citizens to do anything from raise issues to participate in crafting policy. The agonistic spirit of online debate would be promoted through different mechanisms which could be used to express agreement and disagreement, in order to ensure that real options would be presented for votes and that no one's dissenting position would be steamrolled by consensual wholes or tyrannical majorities.

Even with the above as a kind of rough draft vision of how an online layered politics might operate, the big question, perhaps even bigger than the question of what alternatives would look like, is how to get from here to there. With electoral politics increasingly becoming more administrative and narrow in choice and the old idea of forming a vanguard party and seizing power through armed revolution simply out of the question in today's context, the question of how to go about bringing any sort of major change remains puzzling. It is on this register, that the four terrains of contestation between politics and anti-politics once again become informative. If each terrain can be configured to be more or less political, then the idea of an alternative to the status quo has actionable steps. In addition, each of the elements of the four terrains can be more or less digitized. By focusing on ways to expand both the politicization and digitization of each terrain, a progressive reinvigoration of politics is possible. Such progress may be uneven, as digitization does not necessarily result in politicization and vice versa, but the terrains of contestation can provide activists with both a point of focus for individual action and a wider vision.

The political realm as a common space for political speech and action presents many avenues for action. Existing websites with large political forums should seek to become more than unofficial discussion spaces and start to take on the guise of shadow governments. By politicizing an existing digital space and turning it into more of a common site where everyone could go to discuss political issues, a political realm that functioned as a common world could be established online. Governmental spaces can be sites of digitization as well. Legislative debates and decisions should be broadcast online, and governments should be encouraged to expand digital means to get feedback from citizens. A member of parliament, for instance could be encouraged to hold online meetings where people could bring up and discuss issues, eventually leading to the transformation of representatives into delegates beholden to the decisions of the constituents.

Participation in unofficial discussion forums can be politicized by enabling people to not just take part in discussions and debates, but allowing community votes and decisions which could influence official decision makers. Adopting such structures could make a whole host of organizations more political and democratic, eliminating the need for leaders and officials. Unions, community organizations, and political parties would be better served adopting digital participation methods in order to ensure their various debate and decision making procedures were more accountable and encouraged political participation. Voting in elections should be available online more widely, as it could encourage more direct citizen participation in other aspects of government. A two-sided approach toward politicization and digitization can be applied by both pressuring official government entities and at the same time attempting to create parallel structures that are more political and more digital than the official sites of politics. Such an approach bridges the gap between advocates of reform from the inside and advocates of acting entirely outside of official politics and helps push each side to be more political.

Even though, taken altogether, the vision of an online politics presented here amounts to a radical alternative to the status quo which would fundamentally change how public affairs is conducted, the focus on the four terrains as a sliding scale of politicization and depoliticization enables a framework for incremental improvement. To reinvigorate politics by making it more participatory and conflictual seems to be a daunting proposition today, but the internet is opening up the potential for a political space and political subject formation process that simply is unavailable elsewhere. Without an embrace of the online world, the prospect for politics is extremely dim. The continuing potential to shape the software layer of the internet in political ways represents a rare opportunity that advocates of agonistic, participatory, and radical politics need to embrace as quite possibly the only way to realistically implement alternative visions of politics. Just as the internet remains plastic, activists such as those from the Arab Spring, Occupy, and Anonymous movements, must continue to adapt and evolve their alternative vision, rather than simply refusing to put forth alternatives, as is the case with some theorists such as Rancière, or simply trying to repeat history, as with Badiou and Žižek's attempt to repackage communism (Douzinas and Žižek 2010). The internet provides a rare opportunity to reinvigorate politics which is otherwise practically impossible. Abandoning the internet as unsuitable to politics amounts to abandoning politics altogether, and allowing yet another victory for the anti-political status quo.

Notes

1 Exemplary works of this nature include: Bonnie Honig, *Political Theory and the Displacement of Politics* (Ithaca, NY: Cornell University Press, 1993); Andreas Kalyvas, *Democracy and the Politics of the Extraordinary: Max Weber, Carl Schmitt, and Hannah Arendt* (Cambridge: Cambridge University Press, 2009); Dana R. Villa, 'Postmodernism and the Public Sphere,' *American Political Science Review* 86, no. 3 (1992): 712–21.

2 See (Arendt 1998, 199) Here she states that the those traditionally excluded from the political realm, such as the slave, foreigner, and barbarian in antiquity, the labourer and craftsman in the Middle Ages, and the jobholder and businessman today, simply do not live in the world of politics, and although they may be capable of political speech, she provides no substantial theoretical account of how it might be a political act to overcome such exclusions from politics.

3 Žižek for instance makes the argument that without seeing others, we cannot build solidarity and are more likely to treat others as objects, see: (Žižek 2007)

4 Rancière categorizes the anti-political logic into three regime types. Archipolitics replaces politics with a rigidly ordered hierarchy of parts, parapolitics displaces political dispute into competition for offices, and metapolitics seeks to position the political as an ideological cover for the 'real' dispute at the level of the economy. See (Rancière 1999, Chapter 4)

5   For historical background on Anonymous see: (Knappenberger 2012; G. Coleman 2014)

6   See (Easley 1996), for a discussion of how Mary Ann Evans adopted the pseudonym George Eliot in order to 'resist culturally imposed notions of gendered writing'(p. 145).

7   See for example the pseudonymously written (Ibn Warraq 1995; *The Economist* 2012) for background on pseudonymous ex-Muslim bloggers.

8   Thomas Jefferson worried that 'the abstract political system of democracy lacked concrete organs,' making this body without organs much more problematic than how Deleuze and Guattari posit their body without organs. Cited in (Arendt 2006b, 227)

9   See for example: (Cafferty 2012)

10   Such critics tend to ignore the question of what could be created on the internet, while focusing on demonstrating how current uses of the internet are less than political, see for example: (Dean 2009; Chaves 2010; McChesney 2013; Morozov 2011)

11   These observations come from my experience in the alterglobalization movement. A similar experience is recounted by Bookchin in the context of the 1970s antinuclear movement, see (Bookchin 1995, 14–15)

12   For an overview of these various strategies and their effectiveness see: (Herring et al. 2002)

References

Abulof, Uriel. 2011. 'What Is the Arab Third Estate?' *Huffington Post*. March 10. http://www.huffingtonpost.com/uriel-abulof/what-is-the-arab-third-es_b_832628.html?

Agamben, Giorgio. 1998. *Homo Sacer: Sovereign Power and Bare Life*. Translated by Daniel Heller-Roazen. Meridian. Stanford, CA: Stanford University Press.

Alexander, Jeffrey C. 2011. *Performative Revolution in Egypt: An Essay in Cultural Power*. London: Bloomsbury.

Alfonso, Fernando. 2014. 'Meet the Reddit Power User Who Helped Bring down R/technology.' *The Daily Dot*, 22 April. http://www.dailydot.com/politics/reddit-maxwellhill-moderator-technology-flaw/.

Althusser, Louis. 2008. *On Ideology*. Translated by Ben Brewster. London: Verso.

Amichai-Hamburger, Yair, Galit Wainapel, and Shaul Fox. 2002. "'On the Internet No One Knows I'm an Introvert': Extroversion, Neuroticism, and Internet Interaction.' *CyberPsychology & Behavior* 5 (2): 125–28.

Anderson, Ashley A., Dominique Brossard, Dietram A. Scheufele, Michael A. Xenos, and Peter Ladwig. 2014. 'The "Nasty Effect": Online Incivility and Risk Perceptions of Emerging Technologies.' *Journal of Computer-Mediated Communication* 19 (3): 373–87.

Arendt, Hannah. 1981. *The Life of the Mind*. San Diego, CA: Hartcourt.

———. 1998. *The Human Condition*. Chicago, IL: University of Chicago Press.

———. 2006a. *Between Past and Future: Eight Exercises in Political Thought*. New York: Penguin Books.

———. 2006b. *On Revolution*. New York: Penguin Books.

———. 2007. *The Promise of Politics*. Edited by Jerome Kohn. New York: Schocken Books.

Aristotle. 1985. *The Politics*. Translated by Carnes Lord. Chicago, IL: University of Chicago Press.

Atton, Chris. 2006. 'Far-Right Media on the Internet: Culture, Discourse and Power.' *New Media & Society*. 8 (4): 573–587.

Auerbach, David. 2014. 'Does Reddit Have a Transparency Problem?' *Slate*, 9 October. http://www.slate.com/articles/technology/technology/2014/10/reddit_scandals_does_the_site_have_a_transparency_problem.html.

Badiou, Alain. 2007. *Being and Event*. Translated by Oliver Feltham. London: Continuum.

———. *Metapolitics*. Translated by Jason Barker. London: Verso, 2011.

Balibar, Étienne. 2011. *Politics and the Other Scene*. Translated by Christine Jones, James Swenson, and Chris Turner. London: Verso Books.

Barber, Benjamin R. 2001. 'Which Technology for Which Democracy? Which Democracy for Which Technology?' *International Journal of Communications Law and Policy* 6 (8).

Barker, Derek W.M. 2009. *Tragedy and Citizenship: Conflict, Reconciliation, and Democracy from Haemon to Hegel*. Albany, NY: State University of New York Press.

Barney, Darin. 2003. 'Invasion of Publicity: Digital Networks and the Privatization of the Public Sphere.' In *New Perspectives on the Public-Private Divide*, edited by Law Commission of Canada, 94–122. Vancouver: UBC Press.

Becker, Bernie. 2011. 'Cain, Gingrich Blast Occupy Wall Street Demonstrators.' Text. *The Hill*. 9 October. http://thehill.com/video/in-the-news/186391-cain-gingrich-blast-occupy-wall-street-protests.

Benhabib, Seyla. 1992. *Situating the Self: Gender, Community, and Postmodernism in Contemporary Ethics*. London: Routledge.

———. 1993. 'Feminist Theory and Hannah Arendt's Concept of Public Space.' *History of the Human Sciences* 6 (2): 97–114.

Bergstrom, Kelly. 2011. "Don't Feed the Troll': Shutting down Debate about Community Expectations on Reddit.com.' *First Monday* 16 (8).

Berkowitz, Roger, Jeffrey Katz, and Thomas Keenan, eds. *Thinking in Dark Times: Hannah Arendt on Ethics and Politics*. New York: Oxford University Press, 2009.

Biehl, Janet, and Murray Bookchin. 1998. *The Politics of Social Ecology: Libertarian Municipalism*. Montreal: Black Rose Books.

Blinder, Alan S. 1997. 'Is Government Too Political?' *Foreign Affairs* 76 (6): 115.

Bohman, James. 2004. 'Expanding Dialogue: The Internet, the Public Sphere and Prospects for Transnational Democracy.' *The Sociological Review* 52 (s1): 131–55.

Bookchin, Murray. 1995. *Social Anarchism Or Lifestyle Anarchism: An Unbridgeable Chasm*. Oakland, CA: AK Press.

Bowker, Natilene, and Keith Tuffin. 2002. 'Disability Discourses for Online Identities.' *Disability & Society* 17 (3): 327–44.

Bowler, Shaun, and Todd Donovan. 2000. *Demanding Choices: Opinion, Voting, and Direct Democracy*. Ann Arbor, MI: University of Michigan Press.

Bronstein, Zelda. 2011. 'Politics' Fatal Therapeutic Turn.' *Dissent* 58 (3): 71–78.

Brook, James, and Iain Boal. 1995. *Resisting the Virtual Life: The Culture and Politics of Information*. San Francisco, CA: City Lights.

Buckels, Erin E., Paul D. Trapnell, and Delroy L. Paulhus. 2014. 'Trolls Just Want to Have Fun.' *Personality and Individual Differences* 67: 97–102.

Burris, Greg. 'Lawrence of E-Rabia: Facebook and the New Arab Revolt.' *Jadaliyya*, 17 October, 2011. http://www.jadaliyya.com/pages/index/2884/lawrence-of-e-rabia_facebook-and-the-new-arab-revo.

Cadava, Eduardo, Peter Connor, and Jean-Luc Nancy, eds. 1991. *Who Comes After the Subject?* New York: Routledge.

Cafferty, Jack. 2012. 'Was the Arab Spring Worth It?' *CNN News: Cafferty File*. 12 September. http://caffertyfile.blogs.cnn.com/2012/09/12/was-the-arab-spring-worth-it/.

Canovan, Margaret. 1978. 'The Contradictions of Hannah Arendt's Political Thought.' *Political Theory* 6 (1): 5–26.

Carey, Robert F., and Jacquelyn Burkell. 2007. 'Revisiting the Four Horsemen of the Infopocalypse: Representations of Anonymity and the Internet in Canadian Newspapers.' *First Monday* 12 (8).

Castells, Manuel. 2007. 'Communication, Power and Counter-Power in the Network Society.' *International Journal of Communication* 1 (1): 238–66.

———. 2008. 'The New Public Sphere: Global Civil Society, Communication Networks, and Global Governance.' *The Annals of the American Academy of Political and Social Science* 616 (1): 78–93.

———. 2011. 'The Popular Uprisings in the Arab World Perhaps Constitute the Most Important Internet-Led and Facilitated Change.' *Open University of Catalonia*. February. http://www.uoc.edu/portal/en/sala-de-premsa/actualitat/entrevistes/2011/manuel_castells.html.

Chaves, Elisabeth. 2010. 'The Internet as Global Platform? Grounding the Magically Levitating Public Sphere.' *New Political Science* 32 (1): 23–41.

Choo, Kim-Kwang Raymond, and Russell G. Smith. 2008. 'Criminal Exploitation of Online Systems by Organised Crime Groups.' *Asian Journal of Criminology* 3 (1): 37–59.

Christensen, Henrik Serup. 2011. 'Political Activities on the Internet: Slacktivism; or Political Participation by Other Means?' *First Monday* 16 (2).

Coleman, E. Gabriella. 2011. 'Anonymous: From the Lulz to Collective Action.' *The New Everyday*. 6 April. http://mediacommons.futureofthebook.org/tne/pieces/anonymous-lulz-collective-action.

———. 2012. 'Phreaks, Hackers, and Trolls: The Politics of Transgression and Spectacle.' In *The Social Media Reader*, edited by Michael Mandiberg, 99–119. New York: New York University Press.

———. 2014. *Hacker, Hoaxer, Whistleblower, Spy: The Many Faces of Anonymous*. London: Verso.

[*The*] *Communist Horizon, with Jodi Dean*. 2011. http://vimeo.com/27327373.

Cronin, Thomas E. 1999. *Direct Democracy: The Politics of Initiative, Referendum, and Recall*. Bloomington, IN: iUniverse.

Dahlberg, Lincoln. 2001a. 'Extending the Public Sphere through Cyberspace: The Case of Minnesota E-Democracy.' *First Monday* 6 (3). http://firstmonday.org/ojs/index.php/fm/article/view/838.

———. 2001b. 'Computer-Mediated Communication and The Public Sphere: A Critical Analysis.' *Journal of Computer-Mediated Communication* 7 (1).

Dahlberg, Lincoln, and Eugenia Siapera. 2007. 'Introduction: Tracing Radical Democracy and the Internet.' In *Radical Democracy and the Internet: Interrogating Theory and Practice*, edited by Lincoln Dahlberg and Eugenia Siapera. Basingstoke: Palgrave Macmillan.

Davis, Richard. 1999. *The Web of Politics: The Internet's Impact on the American Political System*. Oxford: Oxford University Press.

Dean, Jodi. 2003. 'Why the Net Is Not a Public Sphere.' *Constellations* 10 (1): 95–112.

———. 2009. *Democracy and Other Neoliberal Fantasies: Communicative Capitalism and Left Politics*. Durham, NC: Duke University Press.

Derrida, Jacques. 2005. *Rogues: Two Essays on Reason*. Stanford, CA: Stanford University Press.

Descombes, Vincent. 1988. 'A Propos of the "Critique of the Subject" and of the Critique of This Critique.' *Topoi* 7 (2): 123–31.

Díaz Álvarez, Enrique, and Chantal Mouffe. 2010. 'Interview with Chantal Mouffe: Pluralism Is Linked to the Acceptance of Conflict.' *Barcelona Metropolis*. http://w2.bcn.cat/bcnmetropolis/arxiu/en/page238b.html?id=21&ui=438.

Dietz, Mary G. 1994. 'Hannah Arendt and Feminist Politics.' In *Hannah Arendt: Critical Essays*, edited by Lewis P. Hinchman and Sandra K. Hinchman, 231–60. Albany, NY: State University of New York Press.

Donath, Judith S. 1999. 'Identity and Deception in the Virtual Community.' In *Communities in Cyberspace*, edited by Peter Kollock and Marc Smith, 27–58. London: Routledge.

Dourish, Paul. 2004. *Where the Action Is: The Foundations of Embodied Interaction*. Cambridge, MA: MIT Press.

Douzinas, Costas and Žižek, Slavoj, eds. 2010. *The Idea of Communism*. London, Verso.

Dreyfus, Hubert L. 2008. *On the Internet*. Abingdon: Routledge.

Easley, Alexis. 1996. 'Authorship, Gender and Identity: George Eliot in the 1850s.' *Women's Writing* 3 (2): 145–60.

The Economist. 2012. 'No God, Not Even Allah,' November 24. http://www. economist.com/news/international/21567059-ex-muslim-atheists-are-becoming-more-outspoken-tolerance-still-rare-no-god-not.Erman,   Eva. 2009. 'What Is Wrong with Agonistic Pluralism? Reflections on Conflict in Democratic Theory.' *Philosophy & Social Criticism* 35 (9): 1039–62.

Fakhoury, Hanni. 2014. 'The U.S. Crackdown on Hackers Is Our New War on Drugs.' *Wired*, 23 January. http://www.wired.com/2014/01/using-computer-drug-war-decade-dangerous-excessive-punishment-consequences/.

Farman, Jason. 2011. *Mobile Interface Theory: Embodied Space and Locative Media*. New York: Routledge.

Fleishman, Jeffrey, and Paul Richter. 2011. 'Egypt Raids Foreign Organizations' Offices in Crackdown.' *Los Angeles Times*, 29 December. http://articles. latimes.com/2011/dec/29/world/la-fg-egypt-ngo-raids-20111230.

Foucault, Michel. 2009. *Security, Territory, Population: Lectures at the Collège de France 1977–1978*. Translated by Graham Burchell. New York, NY: Palgrave Macmillan.

Franklin, Mark N. 2004. *Voter Turnout and the Dynamics of Electoral Competition in Established Democracies Since 1945*. Cambridge: Cambridge University Press.

Freud, Sigmund. 1991. *Civilization, Society and Religion: Group Psychology, Civilization and Its Discontents and Other Works*. Edited by Albert Dickson. Translated by James Strachey. London: Penguin Books.

Fuchs, Christian. 2014. *OccupyMedia! The Occupy Movement and Social Media in Crisis Capitalism*. Winchester, UK: Zero Books.

Gamble, Barbara S. 1997. 'Putting Civil Rights to a Popular Vote.' *American Journal of Political Science* 41 (1): 245–69.

Gibson, Rachel K., Wainer Lusoli, and Stephen Ward. 2005. 'Online Participation in the UK: Testing a 'Contextualised' Model of Internet Effects.' *The British Journal of Politics & International Relations* 7 (4): 561–83.

Gies, Lieve. 2008. 'How Material Are Cyberbodies? Broadband Internet and Embodied Subjectivity.' *Crime, Media, Culture* 4 (3): 311–30.

Gladwell, Malcolm. 2010. 'Small Change.' *The New Yorker*, September 27. http://www.newyorker.com/magazine/2010/10/04/small-change-3.

Gollom, Mark. 2014. 'Google Looms as 'Censor-in-Chief' after 'right to Be Forgotten' Ruling.' *CBC News*. 14 May. http://www.cbc.ca/1.2641714.

Gray, Chris Hables. 2001. *Cyborg Citizen: Politics in the Posthuman Age*. New York, NY: Routledge.

Gross, Doug. 2012. 'Have Online Comment Sections Become 'a Joke'?' *CNN*. 15 March. http://www.cnn.com/2012/03/11/tech/web/online-comments-sxsw/.

Gutmann, Amy, and Dennis Thompson. 2009. *Why Deliberative Democracy?* Princeton, NJ: Princeton University Press.

Habermas, Jürgen. 1975. *Legitimation Crisis*. Translated by Thomas Mccarthy. Beacon Press.

———. 1985. *The Theory of Communicative Action, Volume 1: Reason and the Rationalization of Society*. Translated by Thomas McCarthy. Boston, MA: Beacon Press.

———. 1991. *The Structural Transformation of the Public Sphere: An Inquiry into a Category of Bourgeois Society*. Translated by Thomas Burger. Cambridge, MA: The MIT Press.

———. 1994a. 'Three Normative Models of Democracy.' *Constellations* 1 (1): 1–10.

———. 1994b. *Justification and Application: Remarks on Discourse Ethics*. Translated by Ciaran P. Cronin. Cambridge, MA: The MIT Press.

———. 1996. 'Reply to Symposium Participants.' *Cardozo Law Review* 17 (4–5): 1559–1644.

———. 2001. *The Postnational Constellation: Political Essays*. Translated by Max Pensky. Cambridge, MA: The MIT Press.

Hay, Colin. 2007. *Why We Hate Politics*. Cambridge: Polity Press.

Herring, Susan, Kirk Job-Sluder, Rebecca Scheckler, and Sasha Barab. 2002. 'Searching for Safety Online: Managing 'Trolling' in a Feminist Forum.' *The Information Society* 18 (5): 371–84.

Hewlett, Nick. 2010. *Badiou, Balibar, Rancière: Re-Thinking Emancipation*. New York, NY: Continuum.

Hindman, Matthew. 2008. *The Myth of Digital Democracy*. Princeton, NJ: Princeton University Press.

Holmes, Steve. 2013. 'Politics Is Serious Business: Jacques Rancière, Griefing, and the Re-Partitioning of the (Non)Sensical.' *The Fibreculture Journal*, no. 22: 152–70.

Honig, Bonnie. 1993. *Political Theory and the Displacement of Politics*. Ithaca, NY: Cornell University Press.

———. 2007. 'Between Decision and Deliberation: Political Paradox in Democratic Theory.' *American Political Science Review* 101 (1): 1–17.

Howard, Philip N., and Muzammil M. Hussain. 2013. *Democracy's Fourth Wave? Digital Media and the Arab Spring*. New York, NY: Oxford University Press.

Hutchens, Myiah J., Vincent J. Cicchirillo, and Jay D. Hmielowski. 2014. 'How Could You Think That?!?!: Understanding Intentions to Engage in Political Flaming.' *New Media & Society*, February, 1–20.

Huffington Post, The. 2012. 'Uganda Government Websites Hacked In Defense Of LGBT Rights, Gay Pride.' 16 August. http://www.huffingtonpost. com/2012/08/16/uganda-government-websites-hacked-anonymous-gay-rights_n_1789623.html.

Ibn Warraq. 1995. *Why I Am Not a Muslim*. Amherst, NY: Prometheus Books.

'Internet Strikes Back: Anonymous' Operation Megaupload Explained.' 2012. 20 January. http://rt.com/usa/anonymous-barrettbrown-sopa-megaup-load-241/.

Jurgenson, Nathan. 2012. 'When Atoms Meet Bits: Social Media, the Mobile Web and Augmented Revolution.' *Future Internet* 4 (4): 83–91.

Kahn, Richard, and Douglas Kellner. 2004. 'New Media and Internet Activism: From the 'Battle of Seattle' to Blogging.' *New Media & Society* 6 (1): 87–95.

Kalyvas, Andreas. *Democracy and the Politics of the Extraordinary: Max Weber, Carl Schmitt, and Hannah Arendt.* Cambridge: Cambridge University Press, 2009.

Kirkpatrick, Marshall. 2010. 'Why Facebook Is Wrong: Privacy Is Still Important.' *ReadWrite.* 11 January. http://readwrite.com/2010/01/11/why_facebook_is_wrong_about_privacy.

Kittur, Aniket, Bryan A. Pendleton, Bongwon Suh, and Todd Mytkowicz. 2007. 'Power of the Few vs. Wisdom of the Crowd: Wikipedia and the Rise of the Bourgeoisie.' In *CHI '07: Proceedings of the SIGCHI Conference on Human Factors in Computing Systems.*

Kluver, Randolph, Nicholas Jankowski, Kirsten Foot, and Steven M. Schneider, eds. 2014. *The Internet and National Elections: A Comparative Study of Web Campaigning.* Abingdon: Routledge.

Knappenberger, Brian. 2012. *We Are Legion: The Story of the Hacktivists.* Luminant Media.

Kojève, Alexandre. 1980. *Introduction to the Reading of Hegel: Lectures on the Phenomenology of Spirit.* Translated by James H. Nichols Jr. Agora Paperback Editions. Ithaca, NY: Cornell University Press.

Krishnan, Manisha. 2013. 'Are Anti-Fluoridation Activists Coming to Your Town?' *Maclean's,* 9 February. http://www.macleans.ca/news/canada/something-in-the-water/.

Lacan, Jacques. 1981. *The Four Fundamental Concepts of Psychoanalysis: Book XI.* Translated by Alan Sheridan. New York, NY: Norton.

Laclau, Ernesto. 2005. *On Populist Reason.* London: Verso.

LeDuc, Lawrence. 2011. 'Electoral Reform and Direct Democracy in Canada: When Citizens Become Involved.' *West European Politics* 34 (3): 551–67.

Lefebvre, Henri. 2000. *The Production of Space.* Translated by Donald Nicholson-Smith. Malden, MA: Blackwell.

Lessig, Lawrence. 2006. *Code: Version 2.0.* New York, NY: Basic Books.

Locke, John. 2003. *Two Treatises of Government, And; A Letter Concerning Toleration.* New Haven, CT: Yale University Press.

Macpherson, C.B. 1977. *The Life and Times of Liberal Democracy.* Oxford: Oxford University Press.

Martin, Chip. 2013. 'Anti-Wind Turbine Activists Block Southwestern Ontario Highway.' *Toronto Sun,* 19 October. http://www.torontosun.com/2013/10/19/anti-wind-turbine-activists-block-southwestern-ontario-highway.

McChesney, Robert W. 2013. *Digital Disconnect: How Capitalism Is Turning the Internet Against Democracy.* New York, NY: New Press.

McGuire, Patrick. 2013. 'Why Is Barrett Brown Facing 100 Years in Prison?' *VICE*. January. http://www.vice.com/en_ca/read/why-is-barrett-brown-facing-100-years-in-jail.

Milan, Stefani. 2015. ' From Social Movements to Cloud Protesting: The Evolution of Collective Identity.' *Communication & Society* 18 (8): 887–900.

Miller, Dale. 2010. *Classic Thinkers: John Stuart Mill.* Cambridge: Polity Press.

Montesquieu, Charles de Secondat baron de. 1989. *The Spirit of the Laws.* Edited by Anne M. Cohler, Basia C. Miller, and Harold S. Stone. Cambridge: Cambridge University Press.

Morozov, Evgeny. 2011. *The Net Delusion: The Dark Side of Internet Freedom.* New York, NY: PublicAffairs.

Mouffe, Chantal. 2005. *On The Political.* Abingdon: Routledge.

———. 2009. *The Democratic Paradox.* London: Verso.

Murfin, Mark. 2014. 'Aaron's Law: Bringing Sensibility to the Computer Fraud and Abuse Act.' *Southern Illonois University Law Journal* 38 (3): 469–90.

Nicholson, Linda, and Steven Seidman. 1995. *Social Postmodernism: Beyond Identity Politics.* Cambridge: Cambridge University Press.

Nonnecke, Blair, and Jennifer Preece. 1999. 'Shedding Light on Lurkers in Online Communities.' *Ethnographic Studies in Real and Virtual Environments: Inhabited Information Spaces and Connected Communities* 24 (26): 123–28.

Norris, Pippa. 2011. *Democratic Deficit: Critical Citizens Revisited.* New York, NY: Cambridge University Press.

Norton, Quinn. 2012. '2011: The Year Anonymous Took On Cops, Dictators and Existential Dread.' *Wired.* 11 January. http://www.wired.com/2012/01/anonymous-dicators-existential-dread/.

Oremus, Will. 2012. 'Anonymous Hacks Westboro Church Over Plans To Picket Sandy Hook Funerals. Bad Idea.' *Slate,* 17 December. http://www.slate.com/blogs/future_tense/2012/12/17/anonymous_hacks_westboro_baptist_church_over_sandy_hook_picket_is_there.html.

Papacharissi, Zizi. 2002. 'The Virtual Sphere: The Internet as a Public Sphere.' *New Media & Society* 4 (1): 9–27.

———. 2004. 'Democracy Online: Civility, Politeness, and the Democratic Potential of Online Political Discussion Groups.' *New Media & Society* 6 (2): 259–83.

———. 2010. 'Privacy as a Luxury Commodity.' *First Monday* 15 (8).

Parekh, Bhikhu C. 1981. *Hannah Arendt and the Search for a New Political Philosophy.* London: Macmillan Press.

Pariser, Eli. 2011. *The Filter Bubble: How the New Personalized Web Is Changing What We Read and How We Think.* New York, NY: Penguin Books.

Phillips, Christopher. 2012. 'Syria's Bloody Arab Spring.' *After the Arab Spring: Power Shift in the Middle East? LSE IDEAS Special Report.* May. http://www.lse.ac.uk/ideas/publications/reports/pdf/sr011/final_lse_ideas__syrias bloodyarabspring_phillips.pdf.

Plato. 1991. *The Republic.* Translated by Allan Bloom. New York, NY: Basic Books.

———. 1998. *Four Texts on Socrates: Plato's Euthyphro, Apology, and Crito, and Aristophanes' Clouds.* Translated by Thomas G. West and Grace Starry West. Ithaca, NY: Cornell University Press.

Polletta, Francesca. 2013. 'Participatory Democracy in the New Millennium.' *Contemporary Sociology: A Journal of Reviews* 42 (1): 40–50.

Poster, Mark. 1995. 'CyberDemocracy: Internet and the Public Sphere.' http://www.hnet.uci.edu/mposter/writings/democ.html.

Prashad, Vijay. 2007. *The Darker Nations: A People's History of the Third World.* A New Press People's History. New York, NY: New Press.

Prozorov, Sergei. 2014. *Theory of the Political Subject: Void Universalism II.* Abingdon: Routledge.

Putnam, Robert D. 2001. *Bowling Alone.* New York, NY: Simon and Schuster.

Rancière, Jacques. 1999. *Disagreement : Politics and Philosophy.* Translated by Julie Rose. Minneapolis, MN: University of Minnesota Press.

———. 2004. 'Who Is the Subject of the Rights of Man?' *The South Atlantic Quarterly* 103 (2): 297–310.

———. 2007. *On the Shores of Politics.* Translated by Liz Heron. London: Verso.

———. 2009a. *Aesthetics and its Discontents.* Translated by Steve Corcoran. Cambridge: Polity Press.

———. 2009b. *Hatred of Democracy.* Translated by Steve Corcoran. London: Verso.

———. 2009c. 'The Method of Equality: An Answer to Some Questions.' In *Jacques Rancière: History, Politics, Aesthetics,* edited by Gabriel Rockhill and Philip Watts. Durham, NC: Duke University Press.

———. 2010a. *Chronicles of Consensual Times.* Translated by Steven Corcoran. London: Continuum.

———. 2010b. *Dissensus: On Politics and Aesthetics.* Translated by Steve Corcoran. London: Continuum.

———. 2011. *The Emancipated Spectator.* London: Verso.

Rawls, John. 1999. *A Theory of Justice.* Oxford: Oxford University Press.

Rorty, Richard. 1989. *Contingency, Irony, and Solidarity.* Cambridge: Cambridge University Press.

Rosenfeld, Jesse. 2013. 'Egypt's Black Bloc Surges in Popularity.' *The Toronto Star,* 24 February. http://www.thestar.com/news/world/2013/02/24/egypts_black_bloc_surges_in_popularity.html.

Rose, Nikolas. 1999. *Powers of Freedom: Reframing Political Thought.* Cambridge: Cambridge University Press.

Rosen, Jeffrey. 2012. 'The Right to Be Forgotten.' *Stanford Law Review Online* 64 (88): 88–92.

Rousseau, Jean-Jacques. 2003. *On the Social Contract.* Translated by G. D. H. Cole. Dover Thrift Editions. New York, NY: Dover Publications.

Saco, Diana. 2002. *Cybering Democracy: Public Space And The Internet*. Minneapolis, MN: University of Minnesota Press.

Saglie, Jo, and Signy Irene Vabo. 2009. 'Size and E-Democracy: Online Participation in Norwegian Local Politics.' *Scandinavian Political Studies* 32 (4): 382–401.

Salvatore, Armando. 2013. 'New Media, the 'Arab Spring,' and the Metamorphosis of the Public Sphere: Beyond Western Assumptions on Collective Agency and Democratic Politics.' *Constellations* 20 (2): 217–28.

Sawah, Wael. 2013. 'Has the Syrian Revolution Been Hijacked by Islamists?' *The Syrian Observer*, 16 August. http://syrianobserver.com/EN/Features/25503.

Schmitt, Carl. 2007. *The Concept of the Political*. Translated by George Schwab. Chicago, IL: University of Chicago Press.

Schumpeter, Joseph. 1994. *Capitalism, Socialism and Democracy*. Taylor & Francis.

Schwarz, Elke. 2014. '@hannah_arendt: An Arendtian Critique of Online Social Networks.' *Millennium – Journal of International Studies* 43 (1): 165–86.

Shannon, Claude Elwood, and Warren Weaver. 1949. *The Mathematical Theory of Communication*. Champaign, IL: University of Illinois Press.

Slane, Andrea. 2007. 'Democracy, Social Space, and the Internet.' *University of Toronto Law Journal* 57 (1): 81–105.

Smith, Joan. 2011. 'E-Democracy or a Forum for Bullies?' *The Independent*. 7 August. http://www.independent.co.uk/opinion/commentators/joan-smith/joan-smith-edemocracy-or-a-forum-for-bullies-2333180.html.

Springer, Simon. 2011. 'Public Space as Emancipation: Meditations on Anarchism, Radical Democracy, Neoliberalism and Violence.' *Antipode* 43 (2): 525–62.

Stavrakakis, Yannis. 2007. *The Lacanian Left: Psychoanalysis, Theory, Politics*. Edinburgh: University Press.

Stone, Allucquere Rosanne. 1994. 'Split Subjects, Not Atoms; Or, How I Fell in Love with My Prosthesis.' *Configurations* 2 (1): 173–90.

Stromer-Galley, Jennifer, and Alexis Wichowski. 2011. 'Political Discussion Online.' In *The Handbook of Internet Studies*, edited by Mia Consalvo and Charles Ess. West Sussex: Wiley-Blackwell.

Suler, John. 2004. 'The Online Disinhibition Effect.' *CyberPsychology & Behavior* 7 (3): 321–26.

Sunstein, Cass R. 2009. *Republic.com 2.0*. Princeton, NJ: Princeton University Press.

Tamas, G.M. 2000. 'On Post-Fascism: How citizenship is becoming an exclusive privilege,' *Boston Review*. http://bostonreview.net/world/g-m-tam%C3%A1s-post-fascism

Taylor, Charles. 2011. *Multiculturalism: Examining the Politics of Recognition*. Princeton, NJ: Princeton University Press.

Tudoroiu, Theodor. 2014. 'Social Media and Revolutionary Waves: The Case of the Arab Spring.' *New Political Science* 36 (3): 346–65.

Turkle, Sherry. 2011. *Alone Together: Why We Expect More from Technology and Less from Each Other*. New York, NY: Basic Books.

Turley, Jonathan. 2014. 'Edward Snowden: Whistleblower or Traitor?' *Al-Jazeera*, 9 June. http://www.aljazeera.com/indepth/opinion/2014/06/edward-snowden-whistleblower-tra-20146955611522671.html.

van Tets, Fernande. 2014. 'Isis Takes Iraq's Largest Christian Town as Residents Told – "Leave, Convert or Die."' *The Independent*, 7 August. http://www.independent.co.uk/news/world/middle-east/isis-takes-iraqs-largest-christian-town-of-qaraqosh-9653789.html.

Villa, Dana R. 1992. 'Postmodernism and the Public Sphere.' *American Political Science Review* 86 (3): 712–21.

Vissers, Sara, and Dietlind Stolle. 2014. 'Spill-Over Effects Between Facebook and On/Offline Political Participation? Evidence from a Two-Wave Panel Study.' *Journal of Information Technology & Politics* 11 (3): 259–75.

Volk, Christian. 2010. 'From Nomos to Lex: Hannah Arendt on Law, Politics, and Order.' *Leiden Journal of International Law* 23 (04): 759–79.

Walton, Mark, 2016. 'Many UK voters didn't understand Brexit, Google searches suggest.' *Ars Technica*, 24 June. https://arstechnica.com/tech-policy/2016/06/brexit-google-search-trends-tech/

Warren, Mark E. 1996. 'What Should We Expect From More Democracy?: Radically Democratic Responses to Politics.' *Political Theory* 24 (2): 241–70.

Weinstein, Michael M., and Steve Charnovitz. 2001. 'The Greening of the WTO.' *Foreign Affairs*, December. http://www.foreignaffairs.com/articles/57426/michael-m-weinstein-and-steve-charnovitz/the-greening-of-the-wto.

Williams, Andrew Paul, and John C. Tedesco, eds. 2006. *The Internet Election: Perspectives on the Web in Campaign 2004*. Lanham, MD: Rowman & Littlefield.

Wojcieszak, Magdalena. 2010. '"Don't Talk to Me": Effects of Ideologically Homogeneous Online Groups and Politically Dissimilar Offline Ties on Extremism.' *New Media & Society* 12 (4): 637–55.

Žižek, Slavoj. 2007. 'Is This Digital Democracy, or a New Tyranny of Cyberspace?' *The Guardian*. 2 January. http://www.theguardian.com/commentisfree/2006/dec/30/comment.media.

———. 2008a. *The Ticklish Subject: The Absent Centre of Political Ontology*. London: Verso.

———. 2008b. 'Tolerance as an Ideological Category.' *Critical Inquiry* 34 (4): 660–82.

———. 2010. *Violence*. New York, NY: Picador.

Index